202 Outstanding
House Ideas

202 Outstanding
House Ideas

FIREFLY BOOKS

A FIREFLY BOOK

Published by Firefly Books Ltd. 2015

First printing

Publisher Cataloging-in-Publication Data (U.S.)

A CIP record for this title is available from the Library of Congress

Library and Archives Canada Cataloguing in Publication

A CIP record for this title is available from Library and Archives Canada

Published in the United States by
Firefly Books (U.S.) Inc.
P.O. Box 1338, Ellicott Station
Buffalo, New York 14205

Published in Canada by
Firefly Books Ltd.
50 Staples Avenue, Unit 1
Richmond Hill, Ontario L4B 0A7

Printed in Spain

HOUSE IN MADRID

A-cero Estudio de Arquitectura | Madrid, Spain | © Juan Rodríguez, Hisao Suzuki

This residence on the outskirts of the Spanish capital is fully covered in trans-ventilated travertine marble. The ultramodern structure demonstrates the beauty of eminently classical materials, like stone and glass, when used in a modern structure. Though the house has a rectangular base, it stretches out into numerous different areas with some very pronounced angles and shapes, which accentuate the spectacular continuity of the marble facade.

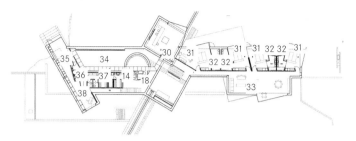

Second floor

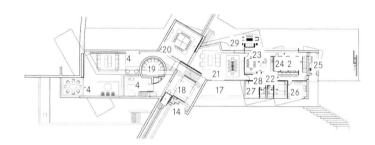

Ground floor

Basement

1. Entry	11. Dressing room	21. Dining room	31. Bedrooms
2. Utility rooms	12. Garage	22. Hallways	32. Bathrooms
3. Music room	13. Painting workshop	23. Kitchen	33. Living room
4. Lounges	14. Powder rooms	24. Storage	34. Walkway
5. Gym	15. Cellar lobby	25. Laundry	35. Master bedroom
6. Pool	16. Cellar	26. Service living room	36. Master bathroom
7. Turkish bath	17. Courtyard	27. Service bedrooms	37. Master
8. Hydromassage bath	18. Foyers	28. Service bathrooms	dressing room
9. Massage room	19. Media room	29. Porch	38. Study
10. Bar	20. Master dining room	30. Library	

001

Frameless floor-to-ceiling doors and windows bestow a certain degree of elegance to this residence in the Spanish capital.

002 If you have enough space, choosing a square table over a rectangular one has many advantages: it is highly sociable as none of the diners sits at the head of the table. No hierarchies are created and there is greater visual contact between everybody.

003 The use of two materials – stone and glass – gives this ultramodern structure a very solid and attractive quality both on the inside and the outside.

PURE WHITE

Susanna Cots | Almuñécar, Spain | © Mauricio Fuertes

Pure White is an interior design project that embraces the concept of white in a house that is completely open to the sea. White represents the colour of the sunlight and the union of all colors, and is the pivotal starting point for the design of this space: a house that is built over the sea, in which light floods every room.

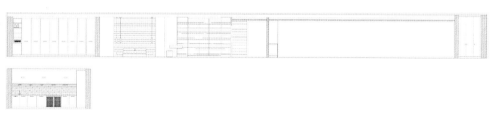

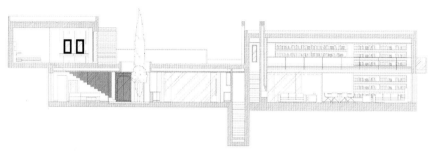

Sections

Basement floor

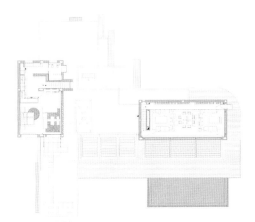

First floor

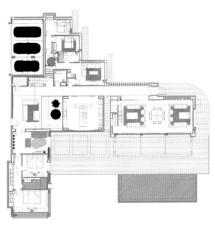

Ground floor

004 Iroko wood has been used to break up the immaculate white of the facade, creating an attractive collection of shapes that give the house great personality.

005

The outside area is designed as an extension of the interior rooms, an ode to relaxation in which you can enjoy the unbeatable views. The oval chill-out bed and cushions add a touch of color to the wide expanse of white.

The living room and kitchen have been designed to bring the exterior to the inside, flooding the space with the natural blue hues of the sea.

006

Defined by a glass wall and sliding wooden-slatted door, the kitchen is connected directly with both the interior and exterior of the house.

007

Together with the outdoor pool, the guest suite in the lower part of the house is clad in the same floor stone as the exterior. This has the effect of drawing the outside in and merging the two areas into a single space.

FLOATING HOUSE

MOS / Michael Meredith, Hilary Sample | Pointe au Baril, Ontario, Canada | © Florian Holzherr

This project intersects a vernacular house typology with the site-specific conditions of this place: the remote island of Pointe au Baril in Ontario, Canada. Due to annual cyclical changes combined with escalating environmental trends, the lake's water levels vary drastically from one month to another and from one year to the next. Therefore, adapting the house to this constant dynamic change, the architects designed a house that floats atop a structure of steel pontoons that allows it to fluctuate along with the lake.

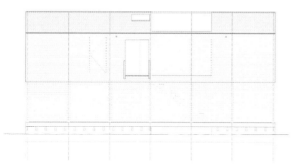

North elevation

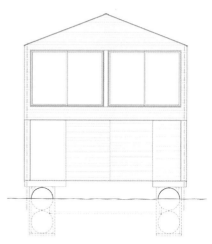

East elevation

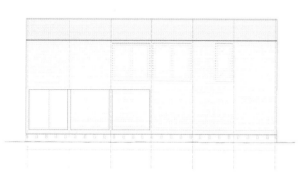

South elevation

West elevation

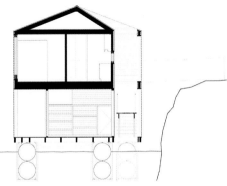

Cross section through stairs

008 The formal envelope of this remote house experiments with the cedar siding of the vernacular home. This familiar form encloses the interior living space as well as the exterior space and open voids, which allow direct engagement with the lake.

009 A "rain screen" envelope of cedar strips condenses to shelter the interior. It expands to either filter light or screen and enclose the interior, while reducing wind load and heat gain.

010 To keep costs down, most of the elements of this floating house were prefabricated and constructed in a fabrication shop located on the lake shore and towed to the site.

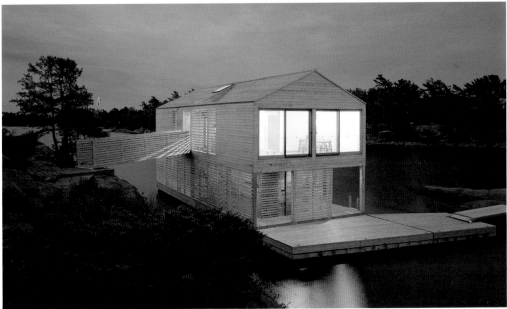

A steel platform structure with incorporated pontoons was built first and towed to the lake outside the workshop. The house traveled a total distance of approximately 50 miles (80 km) on the lake.

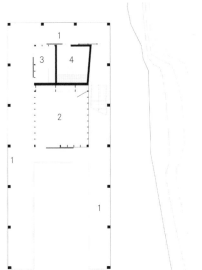

Ground floor

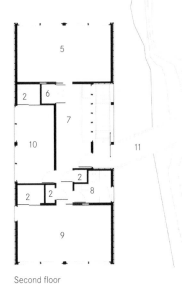

Second floor

1. Dock
2. Storage
3. Powder room
4. Sauna
5. Lounge
6. Storeroom
7. Kitchen
8. Bathroom
9. Bedroom
10. Office
11. Bridge

VILLA BLÅBÄR

pS Arkitektur | Nacka, Sweden | © Jason Strong

In a rocky hollow of a sunny forest, this house is supported on cement blocks and leverages the gradient to provide privacy and isolation. The long and narrow plan follows the natural layout of the field. The dark uniform exterior contrasts with the white and bright colours of the interior.

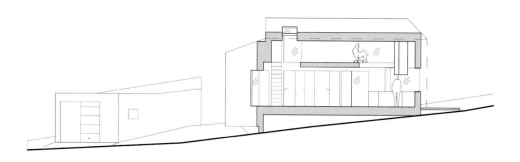

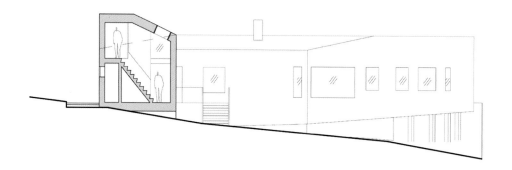

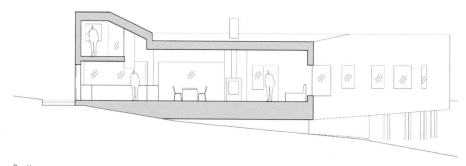

Sections

011 Space, bold design and wonderful views of a lush forest were the starting point from which this house was developed. Hence, all the rooms have large windows and French doors in order to enjoy this privileged environment.

012 The pine wood floor adds warmth to the interior of the house in which white undeniably dominates.

013 Cupboards, lighting and sockets are embedded in the walls and ceiling to create a clean, uniform image.

Floor plan

014 The bathtub has been placed in front of a large window so as to enjoy the views at the same time as taking a relaxing bath. The window glass is partly decorated with circles of varying size etched into the glass, as though they were soap bubbles, creating a dimmed or blurred view of the interior and thus managing to retain the room's privacy.

VILLA MAARSINGH

Onix | Leeuwarden, The Netherlands | © SAPH, Rob de Jong

This detached home sits on a diamond-shaped lot at the entrance of an island in the north of the Netherlands. It was designed for two psychologists and their children and won a local architecture award in 2006. The house reveals itself as a contemporary building and is free of any architectural influences. As the owners work from home, they became involved in the design and helped create a place where the unfathomable could be experienced.

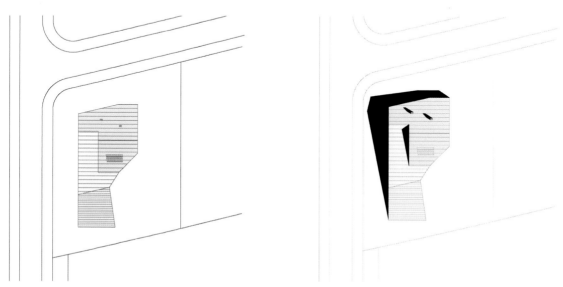

Site plan and site plan with shadow

015 A stacking of plateaus makes up the design of the house. Every level constitutes a different activity and lets the occupant experience something of the action on the other levels.

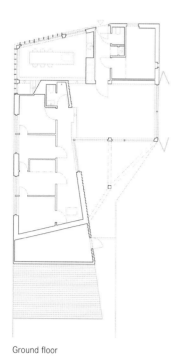

Ground floor

Second floor

016 The kitchen/living room sits 16 inches (40 cm) above street level and forms a link between the children's play area and the work space at the top of the stairs.

There are no architectural ornaments or references to any architectural movements in the composition of this house. The house speaks for itself, and the design and construction reflect the here and now.

First floor

MARACANÃ HOUSE

Terra e Tuma Arquitetos Asociados | São Paulo, Brazil | © Pedro Kok

The design of this house stands out amongst the many red roofs of this very traditional neighbourhood. The solid and opaque nature of the concrete is reformulated with a façade of geometric patterns and transparencies, whilst inside this material comes to life with plants and unfolds functionally with walls, floors and stairways.

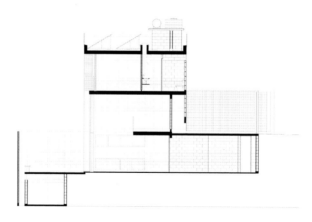

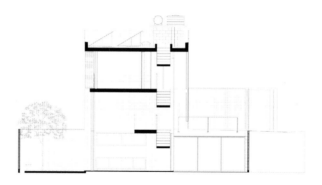

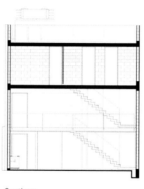

Sections

017 The absence of pillars to break up the space and the lack of central columns in the sliding doors breaks down the boundaries between the building and its exterior surroundings, creating an unmatchable feeling of space.

018

In keeping with the industrial aesthetic, which is created by the use of cement on the walls, ceiling and staircase, stainless steel bulbs have been installed on a rail using the space between two beams.

019 In a bid to break up the monochrome palette of the space and as a nod to nature in the middle of such an industrial design, the entrance courtyard has been transformed into a veritable oasis with a wide variety of leafy plants.

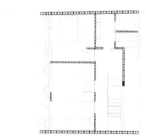

Third floor plan

Rooftop plan

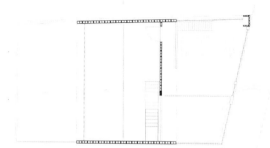

First floor plan

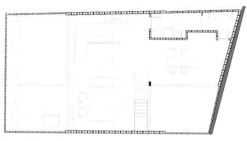

Second floor plan

020 The double height creates two areas: social and private—studio and bedrooms. The mezzanine, at intermediate height, marks the transition between the two.

021 To lighten the interior structure, which is cast entirely from cement, the railings of the mezzanine and staircase are made of steel. They have been painted black in order to break up the gray that dominates the interior.

ELLSWORTH RESIDENCE

Michael P. Johnson Design Studio | Cave Creek, Arizona, United States |
© Timmerman Photography

The clean lines, sophisticated bareness of materials and rigidly geometrical design of this residence located on an east-west axis of prized desert real estate is almost a continuation of its surroundings. Despite the heaviness of the concrete, glass and steel composition, this house seems weightless, hovering delicately above the landscape and bridging over an 80-foot (24 m) wide and 30-foot (9 m) deep naturally formed arroyo. The architects took into consideration the difficulty of building in the desert and the fragility of the ecosystem.

022   To ensure optimum privacy, the night areas —master and guest bedrooms with their respective bathrooms—anchor the sides of the house, while the hearth—living, dining and kitchen areas—are placed in the middle of the floor plan.

Although this residence is designed in terms of a modernist predilection, its bare use of materials and rigid geometrical design seems out of place in this desert landscape.

An outdoor platform is composed of metal grating
and features as an extension off the south side of
the house, which overlooks the considerable drop
of landscape below.

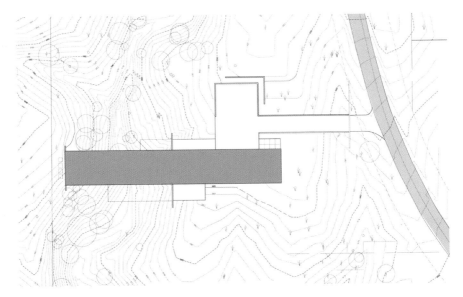

Site plan

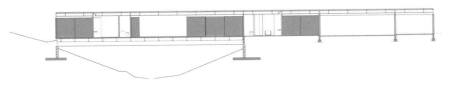

Longitudinal section

The color palette of the interior is kept simple: stark white, muted tones of gray and white Italian porcelain tile that match the decor.

023

The dining room table is fitted into a spot between the kitchen and one of the bedrooms, next to doors that are hidden by curtains that lead outside.

Floor plan

1. Bedrooms
2. Bathrooms
3. Dressing rooms
4. Powder room
5. Dining room
6. Kitchen
7. Lounge

8. Cantilevered balcony
9. Carport
10. Guest bedroom
11. Guest bathroom
12. Terrace
13. Utility Room
14. Driveway

Sun control is handled through independently operated remote-controlled sun shields with variable settings on both the north- and south-facing sides of the residence.

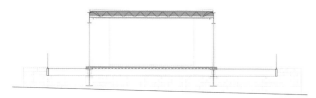

Building section

024

Climate control is seamlessly integrated and hardly noticeable as air diffusers, camouflaged in the lighting tracks, circumscribe the house eliminating unsightly air vents and making good use of space.

LAKE FOREST PARK RENOVATION

Finne Architects | Seattle, Washington, United States | © Benjamin Benschneider Photography

Like a glass pavilion in the middle of the forest, this house has been renovated without losing its original '50' style. The large sliding windows and the Canadian hemlock and spruce roof are juxtaposed with the predominantly cherry tones of the interior, highlighting each one of the materials used to the utmost.

025

In addition to providing more light than a window, when positioned correctly skylights can be an efficient source of passive heat. They also add an attractive aesthetic to the space.

026 This renovation has pursued the idea of "crafted modernism," the enrichment of a modernist aesthetic with highly personal, crafted materials and objects. Custom fabrications included the cast-glass kitchen counter, suspended steel mirror frames, custom steel lighting bars, hand-blown glass fixtures, and various custom furniture pieces.

027 The etched glass wall that separates the bedroom from the bathroom is a focal point featuring an organic design that echoes the natural surroundings. The pattern on the lower half of the glass wall is denser—to provide some privacy—and increasingly transparent at the top.

028 The vanity mirrors hung in front of the large window with their reflections of the forest beyond, combined with the wooden walls and enormous windows, ensure that integration with the environment is absolute.

HOUSE IN LAS ARENAS

Artadi Arquitectos | Lima, Peru | © Alexander Kornhuber

A freight container was the starting point of the design of this beach house 62 miles (100 km) south of Lima. By raising the boxlike main section over the base, the building appears to float above the ground. To limit the amount of sunlight that enters the rooms, several slots were added to the construction. A terrace, with a long bench and massive table, overlooking the sea is the most important feature of this minimalist house, which seems to have taken its inspiration from the country's desertlike coastline.

029 You can create a special atmosphere with a simple play of light without the need for any other decorative element, especially if you are aiming for a minimalist aesthetic.

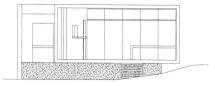

West facade

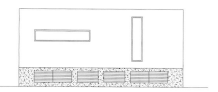

East facade

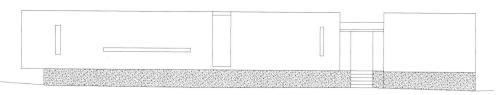

South facade

030 By using simple materials a powerful impression can be created: precise slots in the outer volume provide an unobstructed view of the horizon.

The minimalist design resembles the timeless works of fellow Latin American architects Luis Barragán and Oscar Niemeyer.

Site plan

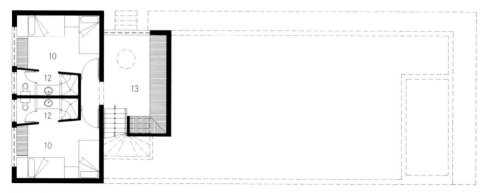

Basement

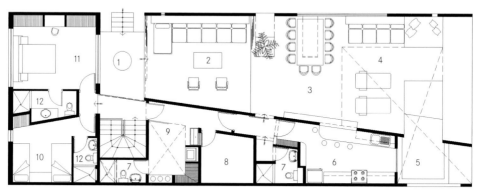

Ground floor

1. Entryway
2. Lounge
3. Dining room
4. Terrace
5. Pool
6. Kitchen
7. Powder room
8. Storage
9. Laundry room
10. Bedrooms
11. Master bedroom
12. Bathrooms
13. TV room

031 Viewing shafts inserted in the boxlike section of the house limit the amount of sunlight that enters the rooms. An outdoor living area is ideal for taking in the beautiful surroundings.

REYKJAVIK HOUSE

Jakub Majewski, ukasz Pastuszka/moomoo Architects | Reykjavik, Iceland |
© Courtesy of moomoo Architects

With minimalist forms, simple architecture and white colour, this house is immersed majestically into the landscape. The distribution of spaces was designed to meet the needs of its inhabitants. The glazed walls not only guarantee the views, but also allow the interior to be cooled during the warm season.

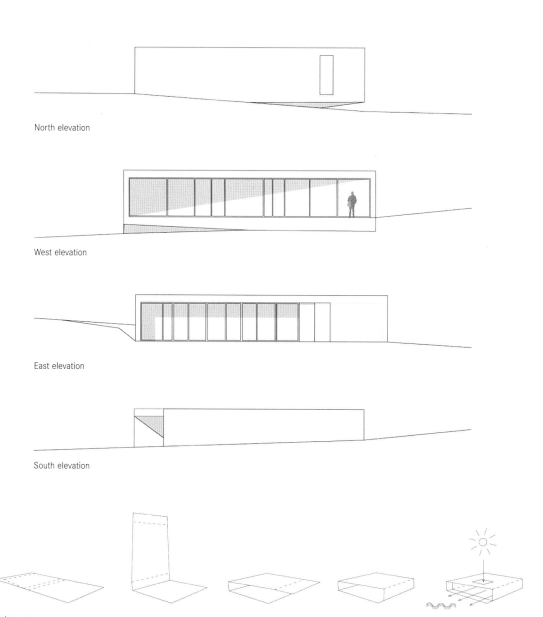

North elevation

West elevation

East elevation

South elevation

Pictograms

032 The floor plan is distributed through a beautiful set of volumes, with large partitions that separate the different areas, the dining room and living room.

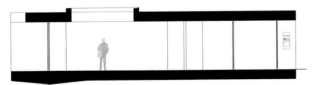

Section

033

To create an intimate and welcoming feeling in the dining area, a hanging lamp gives off a focused and enveloping light. This means that in spaces that have more than one use, a dining area can be separated from the rest of the spaces in the room.

Floor plan

034 Sliding glass doors are positioned on both sides of the house. During the warmer season they can be left open so that the terrace becomes a continuation of the house, blurring the boundaries between the building and its surroundings.

HOUSE AT CHAUNCEY CLOSE

Leroy Street Studio | East Hampton, New York, United States | © Adrian Wilson

This East Hampton residence juxtaposes modern, man-made objects with stunning natural surroundings. The residence is composed of three disparate, yet interconnected, volumes that contain the master bedroom, the living room and the children's room, and two ancillary buildings with a pool house and garage/gym. Traditional perceptions of interior and exterior are blurred in this project as outdoor rooms transcend conventional boundaries: glass curtain walls draw the panorama inside, while architectural geometries foster movement throughout the home.

035 Sculptural staircases, bridges, catwalks, walkthroughs and terraces offer a sense of prospect and discovery as one negotiates moments of interconnectedness on the way to more intimate spaces.

This house is made up of three interconnected volumes, which contain the master suite, children's suite and living suite, and two ancillary buildings for the pool house and garage/gym.

Site plan

West elevation rendered

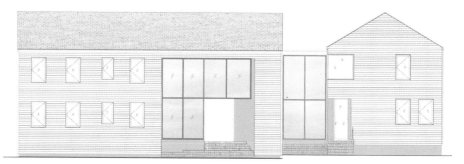

East elevation rendered

The three interconnected structures that make up this stunning East Hampton residence are organized along a narrow swath of land that terminates at Georgica Pond.

036 Glass curtain walls draw exterior panoramas inside and blur traditional perceptions of interior and exterior as conventional boundaries are transcended.

037 Where the volumes collide, interspatial spaces are created, which facilitate movement throughout the home. Sculptural staircases lead residents to discover other spaces.

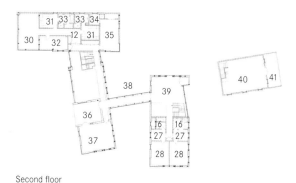

Second floor

Ground floor

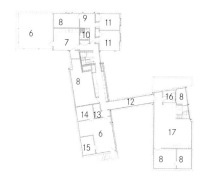

Basement

1. Pool storage	12. Hallways	23. Family room	34. Guest bathroom
2. Entryways	13. Staff office	24. Media room	35. Guest bedroom
3. Changing room	14. AV equipment room	25. Boxroom	36. Outdoor room
4. Powder rooms	15. Electrical room	26. Foyer	37. Office
5. Shower room	16. Bathrooms	27. Dressings	38. Bridge
6. Storage	17. Play room	28. Bedrooms	39. Landing
7. Laundry room	18. Porch	29. Garage	40. Gym
8. Utility rooms	19. Kitchen	30. Master bedroom	41. Deck
9. Staff lounge	20. Bathroom	31. Master dressings	
10. Staff bath	21. Mud room	32. Study	
11. Staff bedrooms	22. Dining room	33. Main bathrooms	

ABIKO HOUSE

Fuse Atelier/Shigeru Fuse | Abiko, Japan | © Shigeru Fuse

The young couple who live in this house in the Japanese city of Abiko wanted a stunning home that would make the most of the 1,076 sq. ft. (101 m²) plot and that would stand out from the surrounding traditional architecture. With radical forms, but humble and open to the surrounding landscape, the main façade of the house has a projection that allows light and views through an immense window.

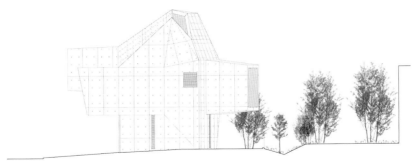

East elevation

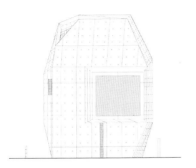

South elevation

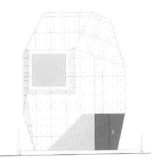

North elevation

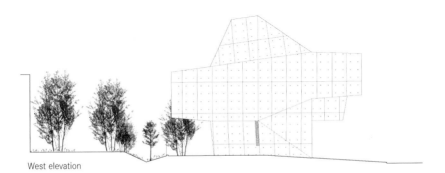

West elevation

Section

038 Minimalist, ergonomic furniture has been chosen in keeping with the innovative and modern design of the house.

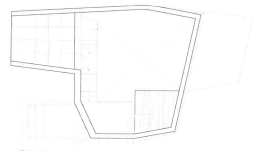

Third floor plan

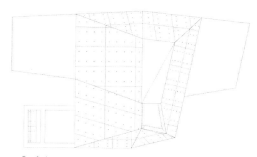

Roof plan

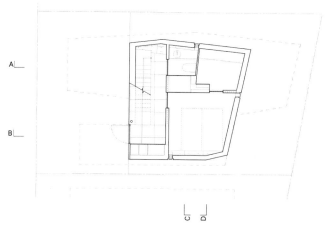

A|_

B|_

C| D|

First floor plan

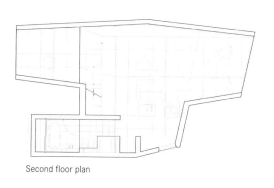

Second floor plan

039 The interior space has been given a modulated, proportioned scale, which responds according to the activities of each area.

A HOUSE IN TAIDE

Topos Atelier | Taide, Portugal | © Xavier Antunes

This rural chalet in Portugal is the combination of some older buildings that were already standing on this piece of land, including an old farm-hand house and a few smaller buildings, and a newer project with thick granite walls. The new main structure is a long rectangle with a white frame that was added onto the existing constructions, thus creating a connection between the past and the present. The modern attachment is orientated in the same way as the older buildings.

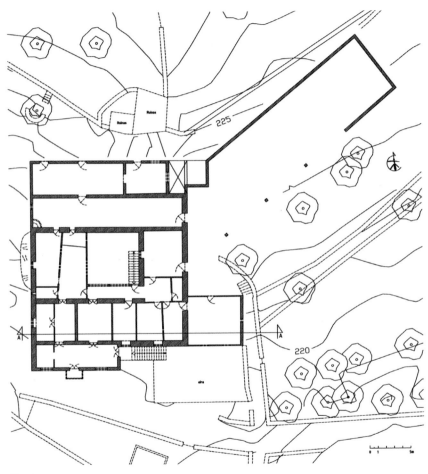

Site plan

The new building with simple, straight lines
overlooks the land and a pool.

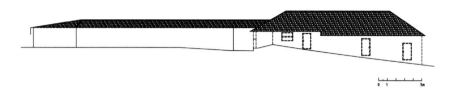

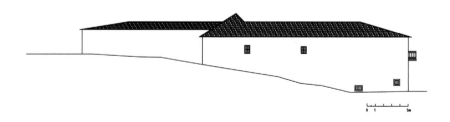

Elevations

040 Old meets new: by combining a new building with the existing older buildings, the architects of this rural chalet created a connection between the past and the present.

041 Rather than demolish the existing agricultural buildings, the architects decided to build a new main building, a long rectangle with a white frame, alongside the other structures.

New and old materials blend in together and create a harmonius flow between the interior and exterior.

The thick granite walls of the existing older rural buildings were incorporated into the new modern structure, thus blending old and new.

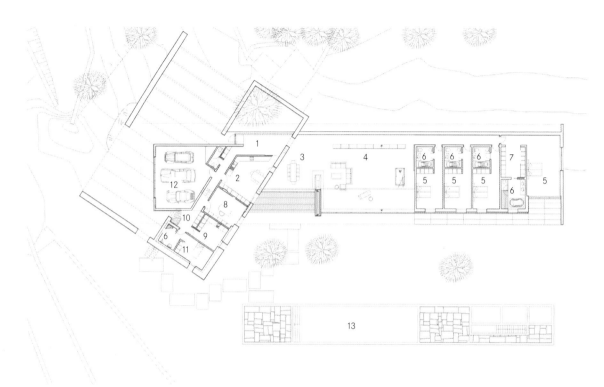

Floor plan

1. Entryway
2. Kitchen
3. Dining
4. Lounge
5. Bedrooms
6. Bathrooms
7. Dressing room
8. Office
9. Service kitchen
10. Hallway
11. Service bedroom
12. Garage
13. Swimming pool

L HOUSE

Jakub Majewski, ukasz Pastuszka/moomoo Architects; Tomasz Bierzanowski | Łódź, Poland |
© Courtesy of moomoo Architects

This house was inspired by traditional Polish architecture. In Łódź, its roof rises towards one end of the volume. The house was completely covered with Thermopian, a plastic material that is normally used for roofs because of its good thermal and acoustic insulation. It can be obtained in any color.

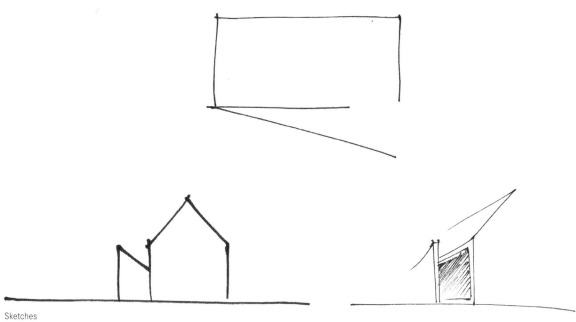

Sketches

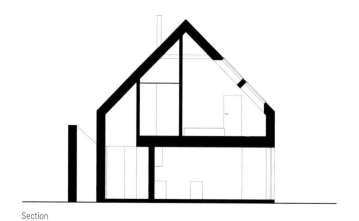
Section

A distinctive sloping wall is the result of a compromise between simple forms and local laws, which require building to be constructed in line with the limits of the plot.

The roof seems to take off towards one end of the building. Beyond this towers a wall, protruding tenaciously at an angle that fits perfectly with the façade.

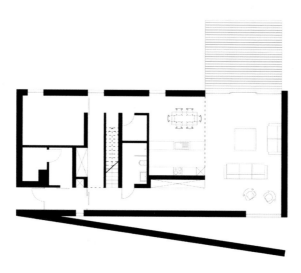

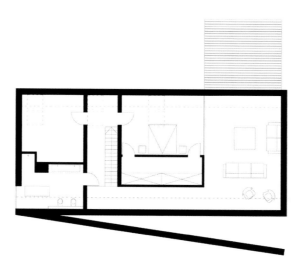

Floor plans

043 One wall of the master bedroom is made of glass so as to benefit from the natural light that enters via the living room picture window. A light grey curtain provides privacy and controls the amount of light that enters.

VILLA C

Holistic Architecturre 50|5 | Zonhoven, Belgium | © Groep Delta Architectuur

This house, located in a small town outside the Flemish city of Hasselt, was designed for one of the partners of the Belgian architecture firm that designed it and it is inspired by chakras and signs of the zodiac. The result is a two-story house built in a variety of textures: a red cedar wigwam with an open fire and cozy Ron Arad armchairs, an entrance and outside wall made from unpolished stone, shell brick walls in the shower and glass doors that open onto 2½ acres (1 ha) of land.

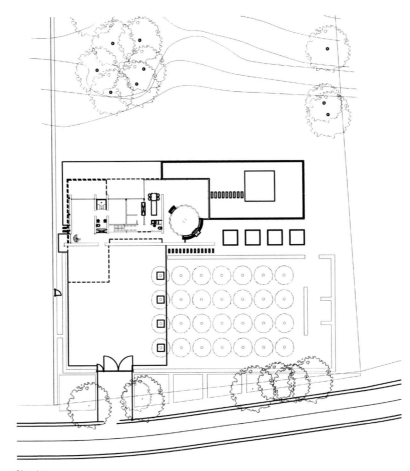

Site plan

Inspired by the chakras and the signs of the zodiac, the architect surrounded the living and eating areas with water so that water, fire and earth are incorporated into this space.

044 The home leans against a gigantic stone wall, which resembles the ruins of a castle. Raw materials and monumental proportions are reconciled with the poetry of the natural surroundings.

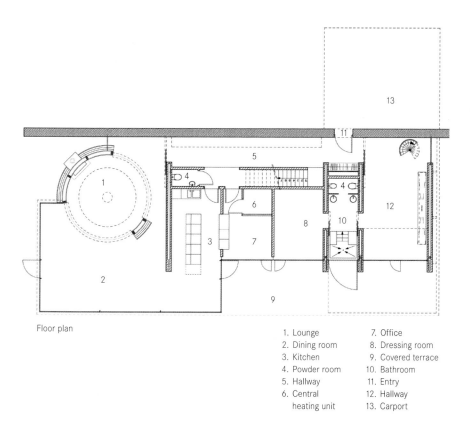

Floor plan

1. Lounge
2. Dining room
3. Kitchen
4. Powder room
5. Hallway
6. Central
   heating unit

7. Office
8. Dressing room
9. Covered terrace
10. Bathroom
11. Entry
12. Hallway
13. Carport

Seven stepping stones (representing the seven chakras) lead to an outdoor living and eating area surrounded by water. The 3¼-foot (1 m) deep pond is used as a swimming pool in the summer.

045

Underfloor heating guarantees year-round warmth and no condensation on the windows. A white, polished-resin floor is as indestructible as the bespoke kitchen surfaces, made from glass-blasted steel and sand-blasted glass.

A corridor that runs along a stone walls leads to an open, cone-shaped back space with glass doors, which open out onto a garden and pond.

046 Far from creating a rustic look, brick or stone walls give a modern and welcoming atmosphere when combined with a contemporary interior.

HOUSE IN OOKAYAMA

Torafu Architects | Tokyo, Japan | © Daici Ano

The first part of a two-phase project for the refurbishment of a 40-year-old, mixed-use, reinforced concrete building, involves the design of the building's exterior and the apartments on its second and third floors. Towering above the surrounding houses, the third floor accommodates well-lit living spaces, while the second floor offers more private spaces.

047 Built on a narrow plot, the entrance is at mid-height in order to maximize the size of the different rooms, which are accessed via the central staircase.

Building section

This kitchen is made of a mix of different woods on drawer and door fronts. Stainless steel handles and knobs are the unifying elements of this creative kitchen.

048

In order to provide visual order to the spaces, white was chosen for all the walls while wood was chosen for the floor, enhancing the feeling of a continuous space. It implements a flexible design, in which the boundaries between the structure and the furnishings are blurred.

049

This freestanding cube incorporating a stair and a closet was designed to avoid the compartmentalization of an open plan. Its location helps to organize circulation.

McCUE RESIDENCE

Michael P. Johnson Design Studio | Phoenix, Arizona, United States |
© Bill Timmerman Photography

The renovation and enlargement of this building from the 1950s presented a number of difficulties as well as irregularities in the flooring and problems on the facade. The enlargement is centered on a new lounge area, which connects with the kitchen and accesses a newly built patio through a large window. Despite a small budget and the use of modest materials such as steel and porcelain tiles, the architects have managed to be creative with this add-on.

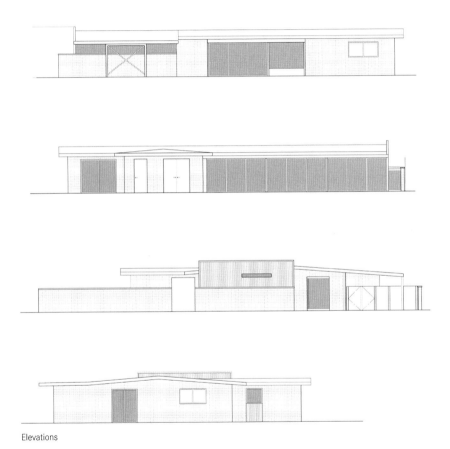

Elevations

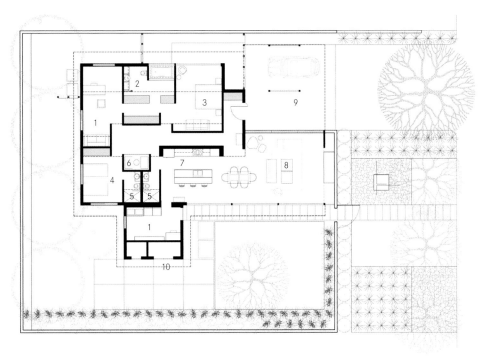

Floor plan

1. Office
2. Master bathroom
3. Master bedroom
4. Guest bedroom
5. Bathroom
6. Mechanical
7. Kitchen
8. Lounge
9. Carport
10. Courtyard

050 This add-on carried out on a residence dating from the 1950s and located in the central area of Phoenix, Arizona, was orientated toward the south to help take maximum advantage of the hours of sunlight.

The renovation and enlargement of a mid-20th-century building posed several difficulties, such as the irregularities in the flooring and problems on the facade.

051 The wall that connects the room with the new patio is orientated toward the south and connected with the new patio through large sliding glass doors, which also help illuminate the interior of the residence.

052 Galvanized corrugated steel was used for the covering and is visible from the inside of the house, thus accentuating the modernity of the interiors.

Modest materials were considered for this project, such as 11¾ x 11¾-inch (30 x 30 cm) porcelain tiles for the floor, galvanized corrugated steel for the covering and glass sliding doors to connect the space with the patio.

SENTOSA HOUSE

Nicholas Burns | Sentosa, Singapore | © Patrick Bingham-Hall

This house on the island of Sentosa is designed to adapt to a wide variety of uses and remain impervious to the rapid changes of the island. Wide-open, interactive, flexible spaces await behind a façade with large windows and balconies. The space is configured to make the most of the views whilst maximizing privacy.

Front elevation

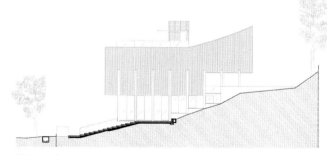

Side elevation

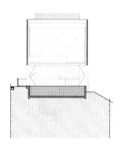

Rear elevation

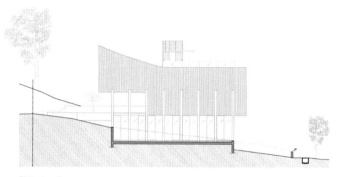

Side elevation

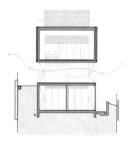

Cross section

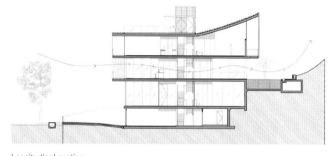

Longitudinal section

053

The structure of the house is expressed to its bare bones, emphasizing the interconnection of the different architectural elements. This design strategy is aimed at providing logic and order at all scale. All living spaces surround a service core that provides structure, vertical circulation, and utility rooms to optimize efficiency.

Teak wood and concrete provide the base materials for the interior. Every detail exudes warmth and modernity in this design.

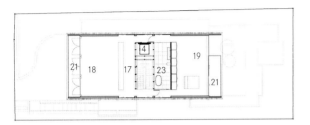

Fourth floor plan

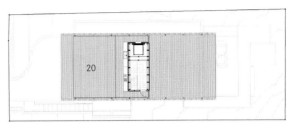

Roof terrace floor plan

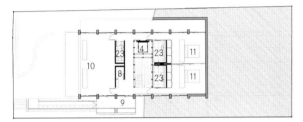

Second floor plan

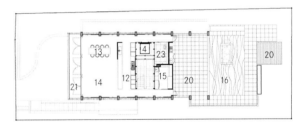

Third floor plan

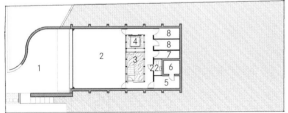

Ground floor plan

1. Driveway
2. Garage
3. Reflection pond
4. Elevator
5. Plant
6. Cellar
7. Pool plant
8. Storage

9. Entrance
10. Gallery
11. Bedroom
12. Kitchen
13. Dining
14. Living
15. Laundry
16. Pool

17. Study
18. Lounge
19. Master bedroom
20. Terrace
21. Balcony
22. Powder room
23. Bathroom

054 In order not to lose a mini office, a bar was created at which breakfast, lunch and dinner could be eaten informally. It also serves to separate the kitchen from the living-dining room.

055 The structure promotes flexible use and the adaptation of spaces to different needs. The structural design, which uses flat slabs, reduces concrete usage by 25 percent. All the timber is recycled, and the rest of the selected materials require minimal surface treatment.

X HOUSE

Barclay & Crousse Arquitectura | Cañete, Peru | © Barclay & Crousse

The aim of this project was to create the intimacy needed to live in the desert comfortably. The climate on the Peruvian coast is not extreme, ranging from 59ºF (15ºC) in winter and 85ºF (29ºC) in summer, making shade the only necessary requirement for comfortable living. The architects decided the structure should occupy as much of the lot as possible in order to achieve a balanced design that was respectful of the site. They excavated the interior to produce ambiguous spaces that blurred the boundaries between the interior and the exterior.

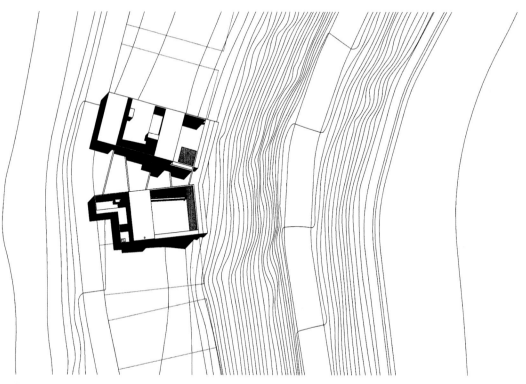

Site plan

This thoughtfully integrated family house is located on the Peruvian coast, known as one of the most arid deserts of the world. The surroundings are natural and dramatic.

056 Colors and materials were chosen in terms of their relationship to the land: ocher and sand tones are applied to the facades to help avoid the weathering caused by the desert dust.

The swimming pool is like an aquarium; the visible body of water is superimposed on the view of the ocean and the arid landscape that surrounds the structure.

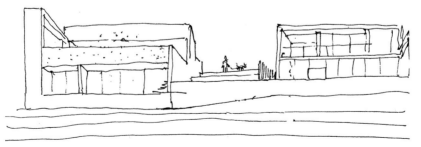

057 A sliding glass panel and projecting roof transform the living and dining areas into a spacious open-air terrace, which also protects and shades the lower level containing the guest and children's bedrooms.

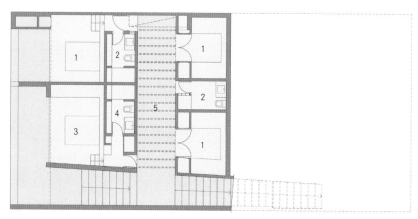

Second floor

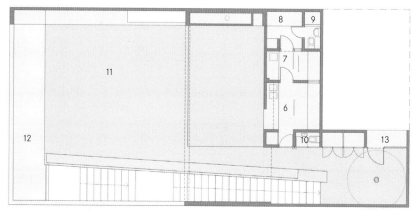

Ground floor

1. Bedrooms
2. Bathrooms
3. Master bedroom
4. Master bathroom
5. Courtyard
6. Kitchen
7. Service courtyard
8. Service bedroom
9. Service bathroom
10. Powder room
11. Artificial beach
12. Pool
13. Entryway

The house occupies as much of the lot space
as possible. The interior spaces are gradually
excavated to produce ambiguous spaces with
subtle boundaries between the interior and exterior.

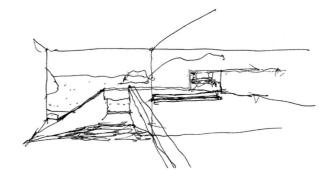

HOMEMADE

Bureau de Change Design Office | London, United Kingdom | © Eliot Postma

This project involved bringing together two adjoining properties as a single family home: the divisions between the two houses were removed, new openings were created and, most importantly, a heart was found for the new home. This was achieved by creating a lined oak box that sits right in the center of the space, from which the staircase leading to the upper floors departs.

058 The coldness of the polished resin floor is offset by the large reclaimed brick wall and the oak cube in which the stairs are set.

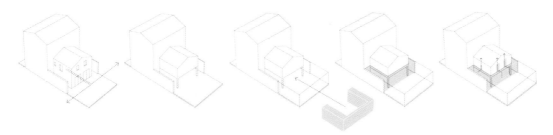

Rear volume diagrams

Ground floor plan

A kitchen, dining and open plan living area was
created at the rear of the property, which opens
to the outside via large patio doors.

059 Independent modules create spaces within
other spaces and can add volume even to
the smallest of kitchens. The classic approach
of fixing the kitchen units to the walls is no
longer the only option available.

Integrating the bathroom into the bedroom space creates an area of relaxation and wellbeing. The elegant sunken bath functions as a piece of furniture in its own right.

060

Inside the house the original features have been retained or reused wherever possible. Hence, the contrasts between old and new, and between light and dark, are present throughout the house.

LAVAFLOW 2

Craig Steely / Steely Architecture | Big Island, Hawaii, United States | ©JD Peterson

Sustainability is an essential element in the architecture of this house located in a fragile and hostile landscape. The house is placed on a cliff above the ocean on the only piece of black sand on this side of the island. Thanks to a 1,400-square foot (130 sq. m) cantilevered concrete slab that sits 70 inches (1.8 m) off the ground, the amount of ground support required is minimal and contact with the surrounding lava is avoided. Sliding doors help make the most of drafts and the wind as a natural cooling system.

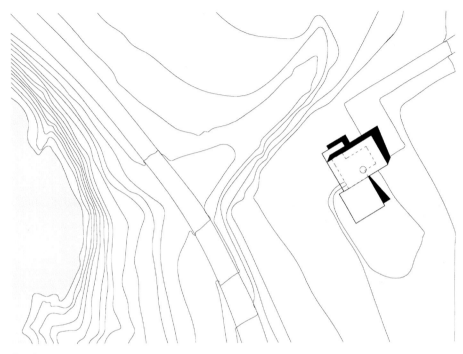

Site plan

Located in a fragile and hostile landscape, the
architects designed this residence in such a way
that it would not alter the land on which it sits:
a volcanic area some 20 miles (32 km) from the
active volcano of Kilauea.

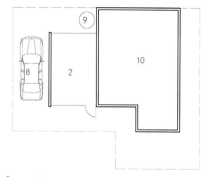

Basement

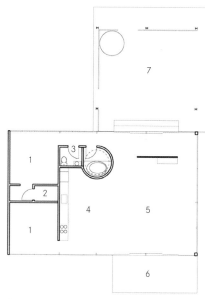

Ground floor

1. Bedroom
2. Storage
3. Bathroom
4. Kitchen
5. Lounge
6. Cantilevered deck
7. Lanai
8. Carport
9. Outdoor shower
10. Cistern

061 Glass louvers wrap the entire building, allowing air to flow while dampening sunlight, shedding rain and offering a degree of privacy when needed. Contained architectural proportions allow the chaotic and fragile beauty of the landscape to be appreciated.

062   A tank collecting rainwater from the gently inclined porch roof is placed beneath a 70-inch (1.8 m) gap beneath the house. Thanks to the concrete walls and shade, the water, which is used for the house and garden, remains cool.

063 The walls of this house are made of glass and wood. Just as boats use wind to navigate and veer, the large sliding doors make the most of the drafts and wind, which serve as a natural cooling system.

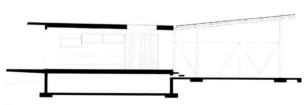

Section

SOUTH PERTH HOUSE

Matthews McDonald Architects | Perth, Australia | © Robert Frith/Acorn Photo

The owners had lived in this house for many years but it was poorly planned and suffered from serious construction defects, so they decided to demolish it and build a new family home. The new house leverages the relationship between inside and out, and all rooms feature views to the Swan River and the city of Perth.

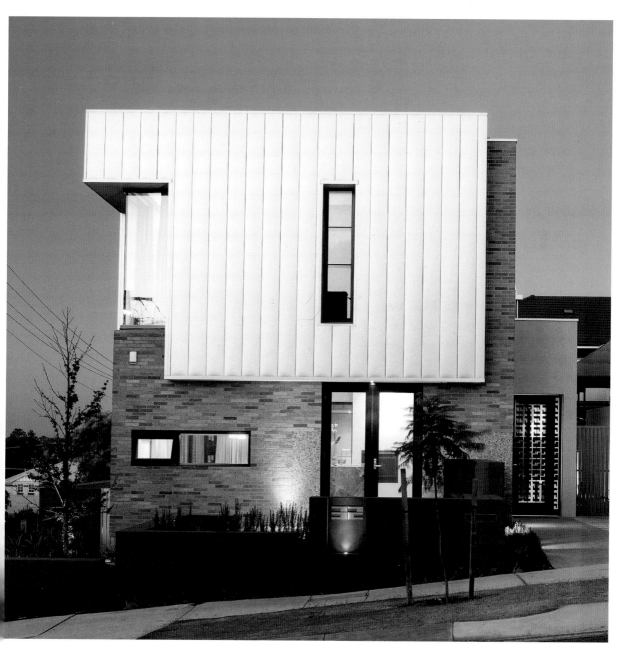

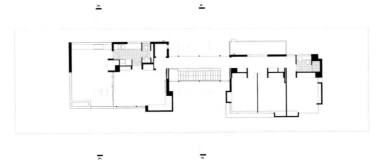

Second floor plan

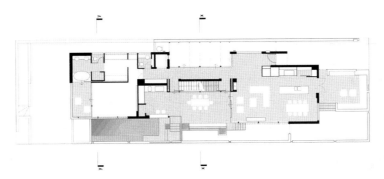

Ground floor plan

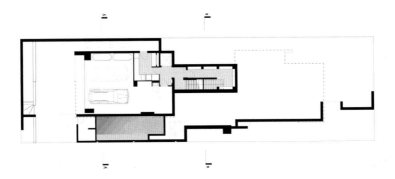

Basement floor plan

A fun pool extends parallel to the facade. Hidden from the street behind a low wall, it reveals itself as a place for secret enjoyment.

In contrast to the traditional houses of suburban Australia, this property is formed around a courtyard with a gallery linking the two parts of the building.

064 To minimize energy consumption and environmental impact, passive systems and initiatives such as single zone planning, compartmentalization and double glazing have been employed along with a considerable investment in active systems. Photovoltaic collectors, rain water harvesting, mechanical shading devices and a hybrid air-conditioning/ ventilation system have been used as part of this commitment.

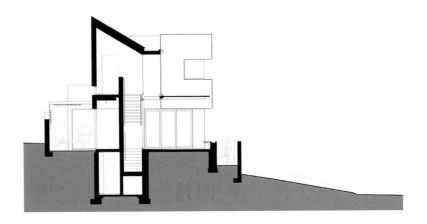

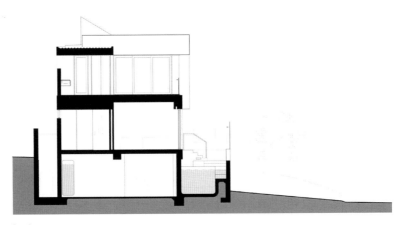

Sections

065 Built over three levels, the basement contains the service spaces. The living and sleeping areas are on the entry and upper levels.

066 All the rooms of this house have large
windows that strengthen the connection
between the internal and external spaces. In
contrast to traditional suburban development,
the house wraps around a courtyard that
forms the main outdoor space.

Admire the Perth skyline from this bathtub—the perfect place in which to relax and be soothed by the beautiful views.

067

The ground floor of the house opens out onto an outdoors space paved with linear slabs of concrete and strips of grass and pebbles. No-mow grass surrounds the front elevated entry porch, introducing the consistent black concrete-tile flooring that travels from outside through the first-floor living, dining, and kitchen areas, then back outside to the al fresco dining deck.

VILLA STORINGAVIKA

Saunders Architecture | Bergen, Norway | ©Michael Perlmutter

Overlooking Norway's southern fjords and west coast archipelago, the site of this family dwelling comprises a rocky outcrop as well as some garden space. The intention of the design was to have just as much outside space left at the end as when the project began. The house itself forms a long, thin structure with a cantilevered balcony at one side. The main facade faces south toward the ocean, while the balcony — extending 19½ feet (6 m) and resting on three steel poles — offers stunning views to the south and west.

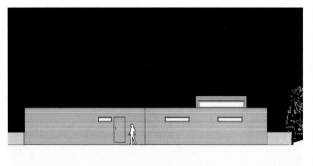

North elevation

East elevation

South elevation

West elevation

068 The three main construction materials used for this project — glass, black stained wood, oiled natural wood — ensure the impact of the house on the surrounding landscape is low.

069

The main facade of the house faces south. The balcony is covered to provide protection from the worst of Bergen weather, while a band, extruding 23½ inches (60 cm) runs along the main part of the house to provide protection from the sun.

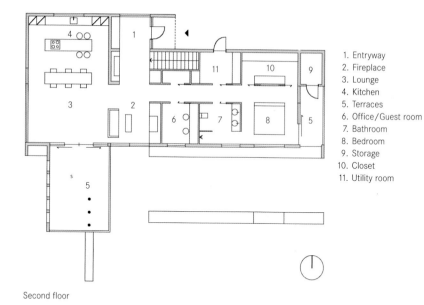

1. Entryway
2. Fireplace
3. Lounge
4. Kitchen
5. Terraces
6. Office/Guest room
7. Bathroom
8. Bedroom
9. Storage
10. Closet
11. Utility room

Second floor

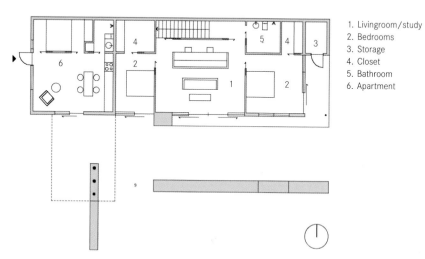

1. Livingroom/study
2. Bedrooms
3. Storage
4. Closet
5. Bathroom
6. Apartment

Ground floor

The house has been carefully positioned on the site and certain design elements have been incorporated into it to reclaim as much outside space as possible.

070 Space was a prime consideration for this family home. A two-tier configuration allows significant open space on the upper tier, which is connected with another open area below.

SHELL HOUSE

Kotaro Ide | Karuizawa, Japan | © Nacasa & Partners

This dwelling in Karuizawa is a clear example of organic architecture: its concrete, shell-shaped structure is in perfect harmony with the environment. Architect Kotaro Ide was looking for a modern concept that would offer protection against the local weather. The result is a comfortable interior that harmonises with the landscape and with the passage of time.

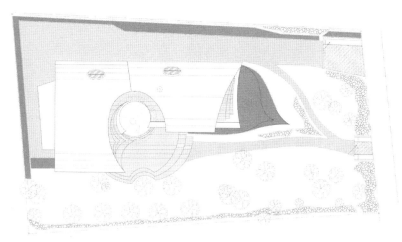

Site plan

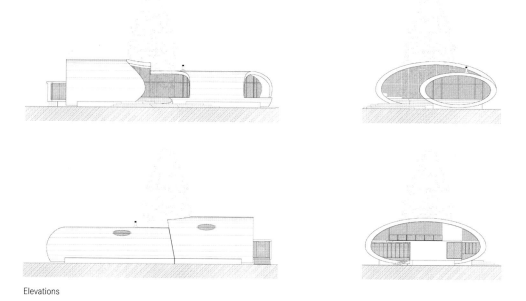

Elevations

071 The elliptical shapes blend in with the lush forest, creating a retreat isolated from the noise of the cities.

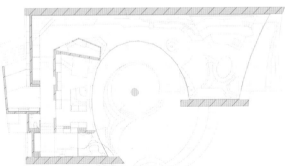

Ground floor plan

Second floor plan

RING HOUSE

TNA Architects | Karuizawa, Japan | © Daici Ano

This cottage house is located in a popular town with an abundance of green about an hour from Tokyo. The unusual structure of the house is determined by the undulating landscape and hollow valley. The light wooden structure is made with beams and glass panels wrapped around a pillar as banded layers. The structure merges with the forest, which can be seen from all around the house. The building consists of three floors: a basement and two floors above.

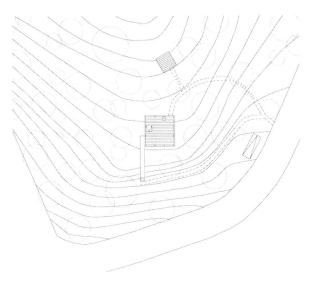

Site Plan

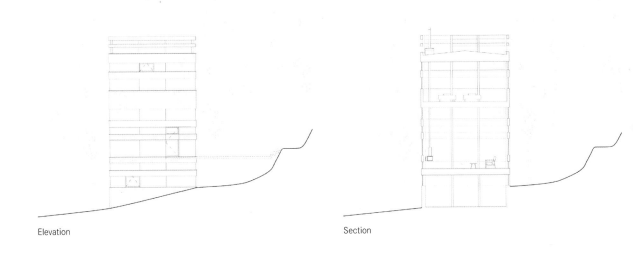

Elevation

Section

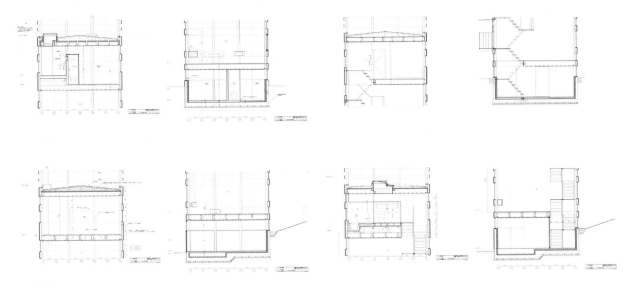

Sections

Basement

Ground Floor

Second Floor

1. Tatami
2. Doma
3. Powder room
4. Lounge
5. Dining room
6. Kitchen
7. Bathroom
8. Bedroom

072 This weekend retreat is designed in such a way that the forest milieu can be sensed and observed from every direction and height.

073 The bedroom on the second floor is surrounded by a breast wall that ascends to a bathroom, (with an observatory bath) and washroom on a skip floor.

074   The leaves on the trees show different expressions when seen from various heights, above and below—lying in the guest room in the basement, resting on the landing or climbing to the deck on the roof.

OTTER COVE RESIDENCE

Sagan Piechota Architecture | Carmel, California, United States | © Joe Fletcher

On the peak, overlooking the ocean, this house in Carmel was designed to appear as a natural extension of the landscape and contains both private and public elements. The large surface area of the house was obscured by dividing the house into two wings, embedding the house into the ground and positioning almost half of the spaces partially underground.

075 The stone cladding dominates, rooting the
house to its environment and connecting it
visually with the rocky cave.

224

076 Interesting contrasts can be achieved with the use of different materials like wood and stone, without breaking the chromatic harmony.

The rooms maximize the panoramic view of the
location: spectacular views of the Pacific Ocean.

077 Walls are positioned only where necessary
in order to maintain a degree of privacy or to
perform a structural function, and are treated
as monolithic elements.

VILLA CHABREY

Geninasca Delefortrie Architectes | Chabrey, Switzerland | © Thomas Jantser

The cemetery, kitchen gardens, meadows and fields of this hilly site are a testimony to the living history of the village of Chabrey. The architects wanted to build a contemporary home for one person without damaging the existing harmony. Inspired by old farmhouses, the architects suggested a construction reminiscent—in terms of its roofing and wrapping—of a shed, barn and the landscape. The house has two different expressions: a rough expression on the outside and a precious one on the inside.

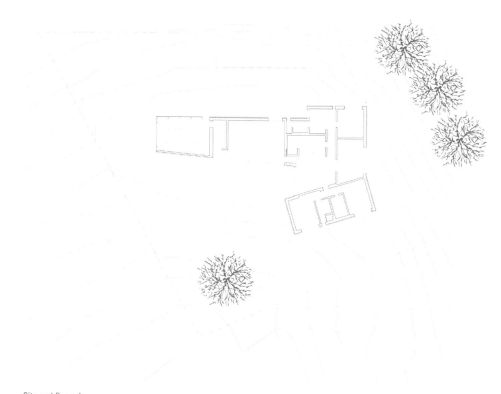

Site and floor plan

078   The house is organized around a central
      space, the kitchen and the dining room. The
      private areas (bedroom, dressing room and
      office), guest room, living room and pool are
      distributed around this central space.

079   This construction blends into its surroundings, not only because of its materials—2 x 1-inch (50 x 30 mm) slats of larch wood—but also in the way it adapts to the terrain and the area's hilly landscape.

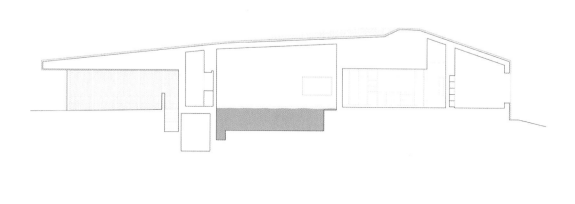

Sections

The contrast between the building's rough exterior
expression and the smooth interiors results in a
harmonious whole.

080 The house is rough on the outside and smooth on the inside, thus blending in with the character of the place and responding to the client's needs and desires.

081 Each room in the house has a special
relationship with the exterior. While
some spaces have an open, more direct
relationship with the exterior, others have
framed views of the surrounding landscape.

HOUSE IN THE PYRENEES

Cadaval & Solà-Morales | Vall d'Aran, Spain | © Santiago Garcés

This house has been built with respect for the area's traditional and much-used dry stone construction technique. However, in order to counteract the compact, heavy and dark effect of the old technique, vertical pillars have been installed, along with a horizontal opening in the roof and windows with panoramic views.

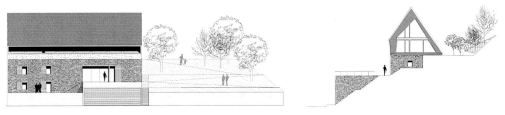

Elevations

Sections

082

There is a harmonious coexistence of old
–in the form of the local stone and slate
facade–and new–which is reflected in the
loft-style interior design with its diaphanous
spaces and straight lines.

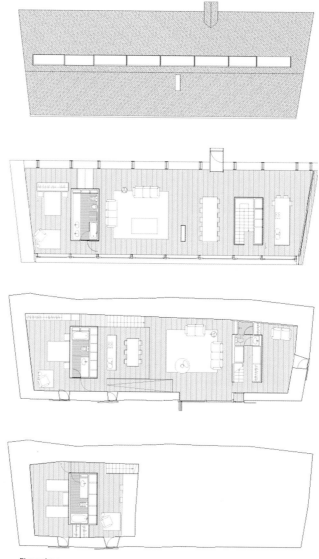

Floor plans

083 As well as being a source of heat, the fireplace is an important element in many houses these days. A double-sided fireplace can heat both the dining area and the living area, serving to separate the two areas without losing the continuity of the space.

084 Thanks to the scissor-shaped roof, impressive height is achieved on the third and top floor which, together with the side window, creates amazing brightness.

VILLA AMANZI

Adrian McCarroll, Waiman Cheung, Jamie Jamieson/Original Vision | Phuket, Thailand |
© Marc Gerritsen, Helicam Asia Aerial Photography

The design of this house is defined by two key elements—the rock face and the views. The property resembles a waterfall, rising from the rock, resting upon it and integrating it into its spaces, and offering stunning views over the azure Andaman Sea. The section that rises directly from the rock houses the private areas, while the more open areas house the communal spaces.

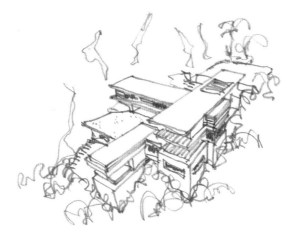

Sketch

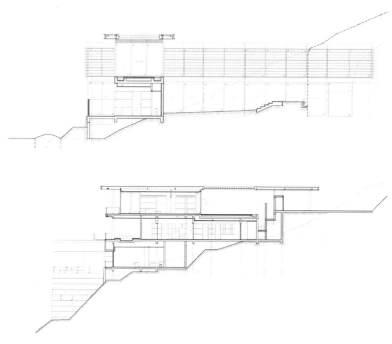

Sections

085 The house is divided into three levels, with the entrance in the middle and the main space that serves as living room and dining room closely linked to the garden, pool and barbecue areas thanks to two façades of sliding glass doors, which can be left completely open.

The bedrooms are housed in the perpendicular cantilevered section that rises directly from the rock and the open-plan dining room and lounge are situated below.

086 The division between inside and outside is gone, creating a daringly modern, tropical lifestyle.

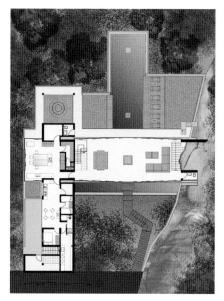

Second floor

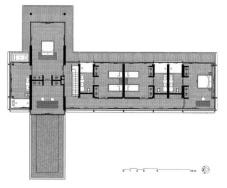

Third floor

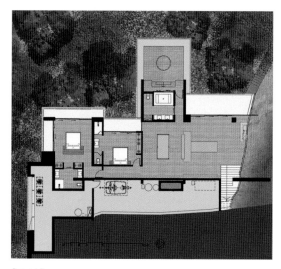

Ground floor

087   A neutral palette, the playful use of materials such as steel and glass in the furnishings, and the recessing of cupboards and appliances have combined to create a modern aesthetic with pure and simple lines.

088

The pool is completely camouflaged within its surroundings thanks to the cement finish on the bottom, rendering the colour of the water the same as that of the sea.

MOUNT FUJI HOUSE

Satoshi Okada | Narusawa, Yamanashi Prefecture, Japan |
© Satoshi Okada architects & Katsuhisa Kida

This house is located at the foot of Mount Fuji in a forest on a hilly piece of land. Sitting atop a solid concrete base, the house relates to the surrounding forest through its wooden facade, painted in dark shades of charcoal-like blue. The multiple slopes of the roof adapt to the uneven terrain and create an interior with varying heights, while a large diagonal wall divides the house into two parts, separating the communal areas from the private areas.

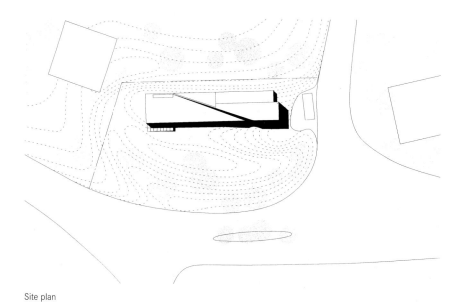

Site plan

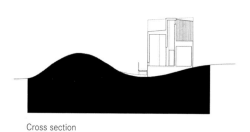

Cross section

Longitudinal section

Situated in a hilly piece of land at the foot of
Mount Fuji, this project is a poetic exercise in
the imitation of nature.

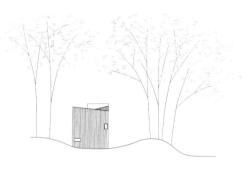

Elevations

089 The wooden facade of this house, which is painted in dark tones of charcoal-like blue, allows the residence to relate to the surrounding forest and blend into it at the same time.

090 The living areas are separated by large diagonal walls, which divide the main living areas from the private areas.

091

The kitchen, dining room and two-story-high living room are located on one side of the dividing diagonal wall, while the bedrooms with en-suite bathrooms are on the other side.

A dark, narrow corridor leads from the entrance to the main living area, where it opens out into a large gallery two stories high with zenithal illumination.

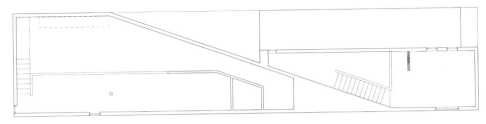

Second floor

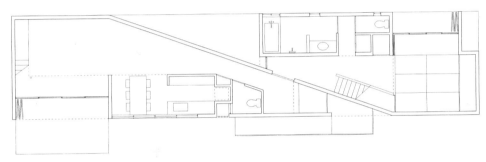

Ground floor

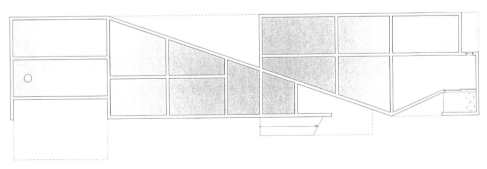

Basement

The kitchen and dining room are located below a small loft that extends from the gallery and contrasts with the two-story-high living room.

X HOUSE

Arquitectura X | Quito, Ecuador | © Sebastián Crespo

Inspired by the minimalist sculptures of Donald Judd, this transparent home is an elegant example of spatial harmony between interior and exterior. The central courtyard defines the different areas of the house and gives its inhabitants the privacy they need, while the rest of the building blends into the environment via a completely open facade.

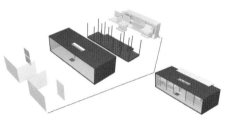

Exploded axonometric

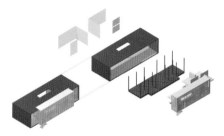

Exploded axonometric

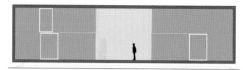

East elevation

West elevation

North elevation

South elevation

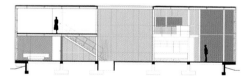

Longitudinal section

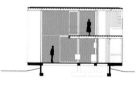

Cross section and stair detail

The steel structure is made of prefabricated
rectangular sections. The interior, with its polished
concrete floors, is dominated by pure lines.

092

A light steel structure set on foundations and a concrete base supports the open box built of marine and standard plywood, and oxidized, polished steel. Passageways, services, walls and other functional necessities are inserted, finished in white, and closed with multicellular polycarbonate to provide protection from the afternoon sun.

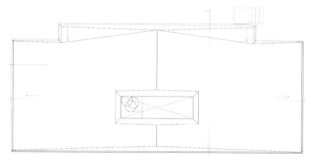

Roof plan

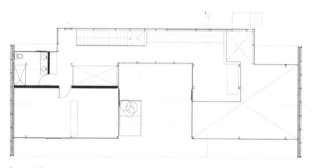

Second floor plan

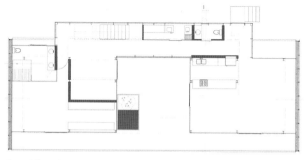

Ground floor plan

093 The glass house is perfect for that unlimited sense of space. The central courtyard offers the possibility of spilling interior activities to the semi-outdoor space, promoting flexible use of the house.

HUS-1

Torsten Ottesjö | Bokenäs, Sweden | © David Jackson Relan

All household functions are comfortably accommodated in this 270 square foot (25 sq m) house thanks to ergonomic shapes inspired by nature. With the premise that the cubic structures and straight lines of the furniture should be very different from human anatomy, walls and interior surfaces were designed for standing, sitting, reclining or lying down.

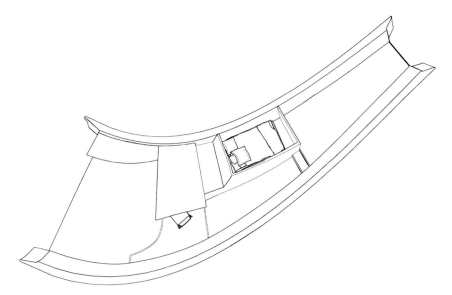

Floor plan in perspective view

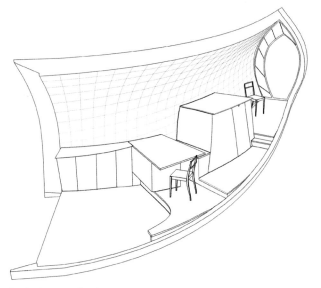

Section in perspective view

094 The structure is freestanding, so it can be moved anywhere. Although the impression is that it has sprouted out of the ground. Its wood shingle skin contributes to the integration of the construction into the landscape.

095 The dwelling features convex walls, which
seam together with the floor, creating a
sense of effortless unity. The majority of the
furnishing is built into the surfaces of the
house, aiming at creating a compact, yet
comfortable interior.

BRICKELL-POLLOCK HOUSE

Hopkinson Team Architecture | Bethells Beach, New Zealand | © Simon Devitt

This vacation home is carefully situated on top of a hill in the Bethells Beach region, west of New Zealand's North Island. Views of the Tasman Sea and the forest of kanukas determined the orientation of the house and the organization of its volumes. The house is organized in three pavilions, which contain the study, day area and bedroom. Many of the walls of the house are made of glass, which allows the inhabitants to contemplate the landscape and breaks down the visual barriers between the interior and the exterior.

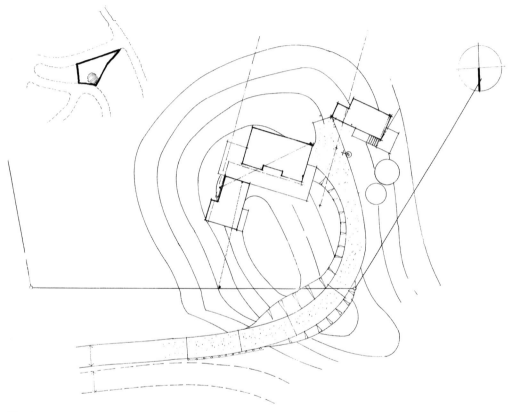

Site plan

Situated on a hill with extraordinary views over the valley and Tasman Sea, this house is an example of how to integrate a simple construction into an exceptional landscape.

096

The dark-colored steel that covers the exterior of the house symbolizes the sand of the nearby beach, which is of volcanic origins. The house is organized in three pavilions containing the study, main living area and bedroom.

097 Most of the walls are made of glass, which helps break down the visual barriers between the interior and exterior. The use of this simple material also helps to create a cozy environment and provides plenty of opportunity to enjoy the views.

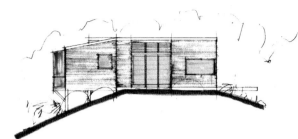

North elevation

ammended 11 nov '99

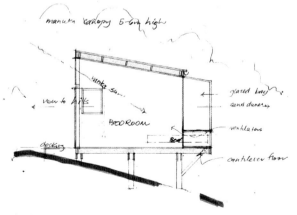

manuka/kanuka canopy 5-6m ht

sleeping bay

East elevation

North elevation studio

manuka canopy 5-6m high

view to hills

winta sun

BEDROOM

glazed bay

sand dunes

ventilators

cantilever floor

decking

bed

Section

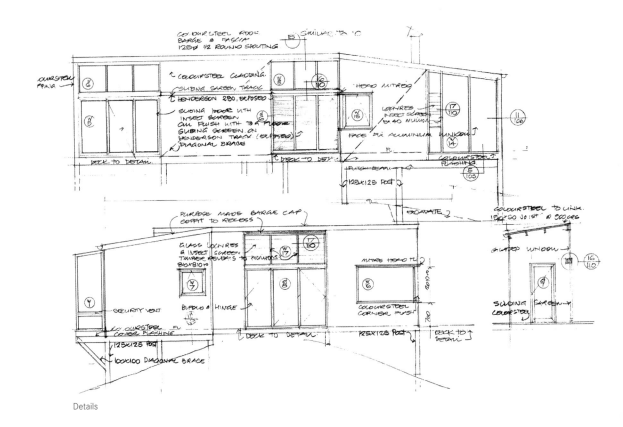

Details

The study is slightly elevated, while the
two main areas are laid out in an L shape.
There are hardly any partitions in the interior
spaces. The abundant use of glass and
well-defined circulation areas allow great
communication with the outdoors.

The bedroom is situated in a kind of glass windowed balcony, with the bed head surrounded by trees and spectacular views, creating the unique feeling of being suspended in the air and floating above a wonderful forest of the shrubs.

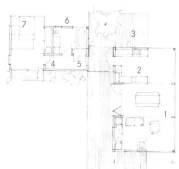

1. Lounge
2. Kitchen
3. Deck
4. Hallway
5. Storeroom
6. Bathroom
7. Bedroom

Ground floor

The main spaces are laid out in an L shape and are connected by porches, providing a protected exterior space. To make the most of the sun, the terrace expands toward the east and west.

MALBAIE VI – MARÉE BASSE

MU Architecture | Quebec, Canada | © Ulysse Lemerise Bouchard/YUL Photo

A facade with a sober and dispersed composition protects the most private areas of this home. Walking through it, we discover its true extent: the lounge, kitchen and hallways provide a panoramic view of the landscape and access to the large terrace, with rocks and logs arranged on its surface as if the tide had left them there.

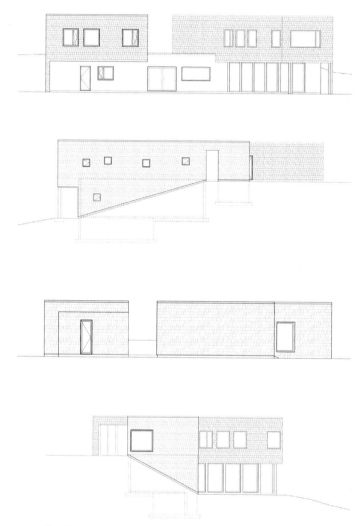

Elevations

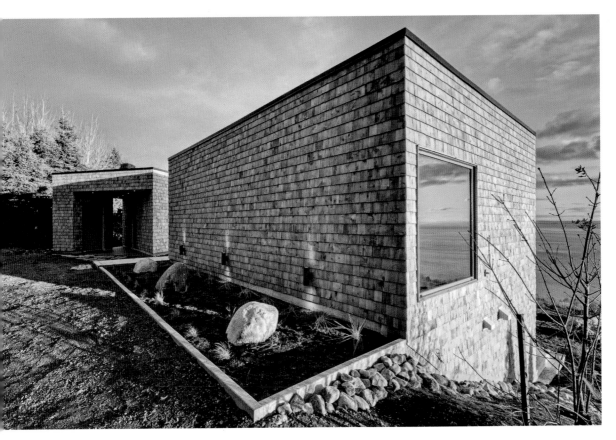

099 Upon arrival, there are two distinct volumes clad with cedar singles. As one moves toward and between the two volumes, an exceptional view is discovered. This observatory is, in fact, a green roof under which lies a vast residence. The higher volumes, apparently isolated, house the bedrooms and the bathrooms. They are connected to a largely fenestrated lower level containing the living areas.

100 The heated concrete floor and walls create a
spectacular contrast of colors and materials
with the cedar paneled ceiling, which gives a
warm and welcoming atmosphere.

101

At the center of the house, a red metal spiral staircase acts like a pivot to the two principal axes. The living room, dining room, and kitchen are linked by this staircase, which incidentally serves as an ever-present visual sign.

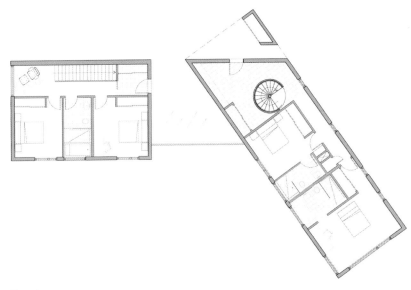

Floor plan

HIGHBURY TERRACE

M3 Architects | London, United Kingdom | © M3 Architects

This project consists of a single story, glass rear extension to a Victorian family house, situated in the heart of the Highbury Fields Conservation area in Islington, North London. What had been a storage area for garbage cans located at the side of previous extension was covered with a glass canopy, which reconnects the space with the kitchen. The entire rear of the house is supported on two steel beams, which completely opens up the ground level. By using large sliding glass doors, the distinction between the patio and the house is blurred.

Rendered perspective

102 Thanks to a formal structural and spatial proposal, the extension of this Victorian house was not too costly: the glass pavilion is structurally independent from the back of the house, thus avoiding large interventions.

103 A glass canopy reconnects an old extension with the kitchen and breathes new life into a Victorian single-family house for a young and modern 21st-century family.

The proposed structural approach creates a visual and physical freedom, and generates a new spatial relationship with the garden, which also modifies the function of the existing level.

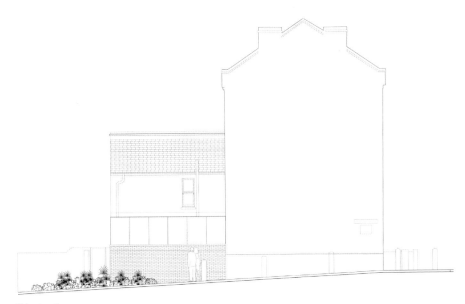

Side elevation

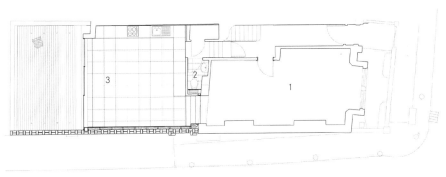

Ground floor

1. New enlarged reception room
2. New powder room
3. New combined kitchen/dining area

104 Two steel beams support the entire back
of the house to allow the ground level to
be completely opened up by using large
sliding doors.

SMITH-CLEMENTI RESIDENCE

Rios Clementi Hale Studios | Venice, California, United States | © Undine Pröhl

This property dating from 1920 was extended and renovated: a second piece of land was added, the common and private areas were reconfigured and a new garage and suite were constructed. Refined cladding covers the front section, in memory of its bungalow origins, while the rear section boasts a large wooden frame which provides shade to the master bedroom.

105

The ground floor of the house opens out onto an outdoor space paved with linear slabs of concrete and strips of grass and pebbles. No-mow grass surrounds the front elevated entry porch, introducing the consistent black, concrete-tile flooring that travels from outside through the first-floor living, dining and kitchen areas, then back outside to the al fresco dining deck.

106 As you enter the house you can feel the
playful juxtaposition of light and shadows.
Picture windows face onto the outdoor areas
and clerestory windows express the changing
levels of the interior, which is created largely
from natural wood and plywood.

107 A bench can be used to optimize space still further. While it may not be the most comfortable, it can seat three people where only two chairs would otherwise fit. Besides being practical, it also has a decorative function, breaking with the traditional aesthetic.

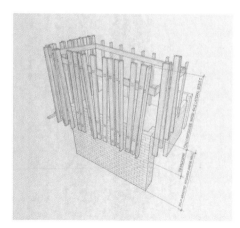

Perspective view of the Douglas fir plank exterior skin

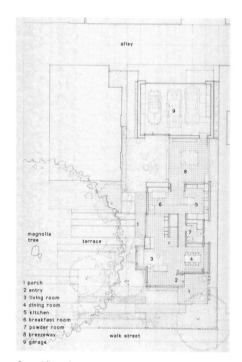

1 porch
2 entry
3 living room
4 dining room
5 kitchen
6 breakfast room
7 powder room
8 breezeway
9 garage

Ground floor plan

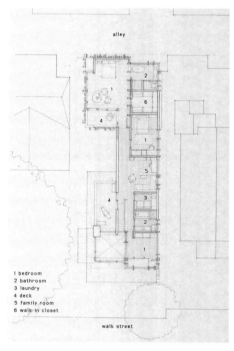

1 bedroom
2 bathroom
3 laundry
4 deck
5 family room
6 walk in closet

Second floor plan

108   Wood not only coats the outside of the bedroom, but is also present in the interior. The warmth of the fireplace enhances the feeling of comfort.

109

Open shelves allow a clear view into the bathroom, which may alternately by closed off by sliding the door all the way across. White cabinetry and positive/negative *faux bois* tile highlight the master bath.

The bathroom is halfway between the inside and outside of the bedroom. The space enjoys a certain intimacy, but also adds to the warmth of the room.

ESTUARY RESIDENCE

A-cero Estudio de Arquitectura | A Coruña, Spain | © Xurxo Lobato

This home in Spain's northwestern-most autonomous community sits atop a 2,393 square yard (2,000 sq. m) parcel of land near the A Coruña estuary. Divided in three levels, the house is built on a base of oblique cubes and walls and covered in white travertine marble. The northeastern side of the house is closed off, while the side facing the estuary is completely open. The master bedroom, bathroom and dressing room are located on the top floor and can be reached via a glass passageway. The ground floor houses the living room, dining room and kitchen, while two more rooms are in the basement.

110

The main goal of this project was to make the best use of the steep incline of the terrain and was achieved by playing with different levels.

111 Built on a base of oblique cubes and walls, this Galician house is entirely covered in white travertine marble. The side facing the estuary is completely opened up.

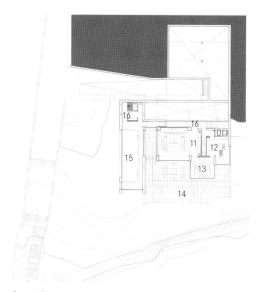

Ground floor

Second floor

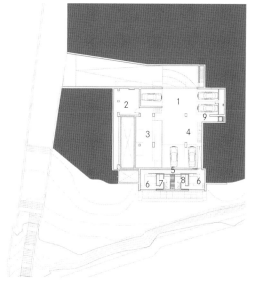

Basement

1. Garage
2. Utility room
3. Wine cellar
4. Stairs
5. Guest hallway
6. Guest bedrooms
7. Guest dressing rooms
8. Guest bathrooms
9. Elevator
10. Hallways
11. Lounge
12. Kitchen
13. Dinning room
14. Terrace
15. Pool

16. Changing room
17. Foyer
18. Dressing room
19. Powder room
20. Study
21. Children's bedrooms
22. Children's dressing rooms
23. Children's bathrooms
24. Children's lounge
25. Master dressing room
26. Master bedroom
27. Master bedroom lounge
28. Master bathroom
29. Library
30. Porch

112 Subtle lighting creates a warm atmosphere and contrasts with the cold travertine marble and dark colors used for the interiors.

113 The house is divided into three levels: the master bedroom, bathroom and dressing room on the top floor (accessible via a glass passageway), two rooms in the basement and a living room, dining room and kitchen on the ground floor.

21562 PCH

OTD Design & Development | Malibu, California, United States

Owen Dalton architects are responsible for the redesigning of this detached house. It boasts spectacular views of the Malibu oceanfront and direct beach access from its private terrace. The whole project was designed taking into account its unique setting and close contact to the beach so as to maximize on its strongest assets.

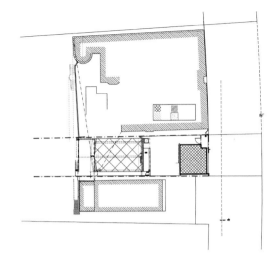

Site plan

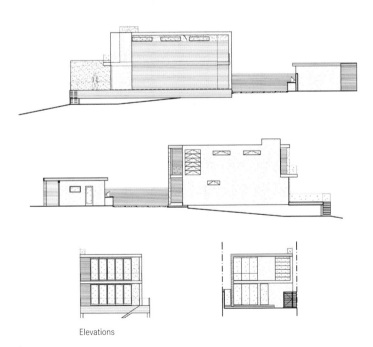

Elevations

Second floor

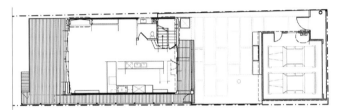

Ground floor

114 The terrace, with its wooden floor, is connected directly to the beach via a staircase.

The interior has been designed in warm, soft
colors against a predominantly white background,
with furnishings that are in keeping with the beach
setting.

115

All rooms have a huge sliding glass door, uninterrupted by verticals, allowing us to enjoy the marine landscape as though it were a painting, providing a contrast with the immaculate white that dominates the interior.

JP HOUSE

Change Architects | Bilthoven, The Netherlands | © Pieter Kers/Change Architects

The owners wanted to renovate and extend this 1930s property. Having studied the house carefully, the architects proposed adding two modules to the house, attached at the side and back so as not to alter the original façade. More than 807 square feet (75 sq m) was added as a result, filling the house with new light and style.

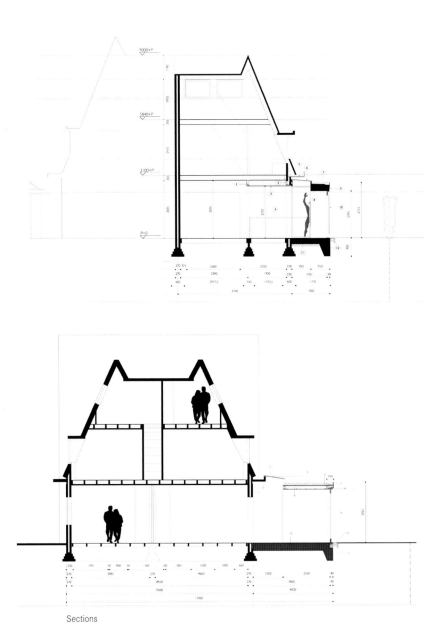

Sections

116   A mix of old and new is usually a safe bet:
the modern design of the modules creates
a unique contrast to the brick facade of this
early 20th-century Dutch house.

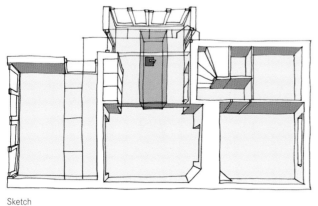

Sketch

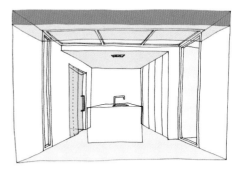

Sketch

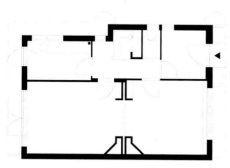

Ground floor before remodeling

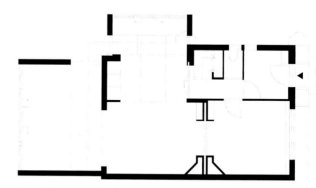

Ground floor after remodeling

117   The search for light is an undisputable force
in the renovation of this house: it is achieved
through the predominantly white decoration
of the interior and the huge sliding glass
doors and skylights that have been used in
the new sections.

118 In a large, open space with no defined limits in the common areas, installing a central island in the kitchen is undoubtedly the best way of achieving versatility. In this example it is a work area, washing-up area, cooking area and storage area all at the same time, not to mention a makeshift office.

SKYLINE RESIDENCE

Belzberg Architects | Los Angeles, California, United States | © Benny Chan/Fotoworks

This 5,800 square foot (539 sq m) residence is perched atop a ridgeline in the Hollywood Hills. The building is a perfect example of an environmentally sensitive building created without sacrificing beauty or budget. Incorporating sustainable design strategies was a guiding principle in the development of the design. Despite budgetary limitations imposed on material choice, the Skyline Residence incorporates a multitude of green tactics for building sensitively and responsibly. The home was built for $180 per square foot (around $1,900 per sq m).

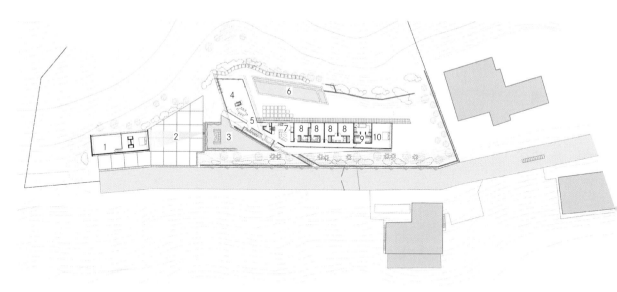

Site plan

1. Guesthouse
   and carport
2. Outdoor movie
   seating
3. Outdoor movie
   deck with
   garage below

4. Lounge
5. Dining room
6. Pool
7. Kitchen
8. Bedrooms
9. Master bathroom
10. Master bedroom

119 Protection from direct sunlight, optimum
views and maximum daylight were
parameters that influenced the organization
of the spaces: the southwest-facing facade
is exposed to evening sunlight, while the
northeast side is entirely glassed to enjoy
spectacular views.

Due to the severity of the slope and the dense
granite stone beneath the surface, minimal
excavating was done. Only earth that could be
reused in other areas of the project was removed

120 Re-using earth eliminated shipments of excavated earth thus reducing emissions resulting from transportation and importation of materials. Also, locally manufactured low-e glazing, steel, cinder blocks and indigenous aggregates supported this initiative.

The house is enclosed by a single-folded surface with infill glazing and screened walls. On the southwest facade of the building, the fold maintains itself as a framing device and offers shade from the harsh evening sun.

121

The suspended fireplace becomes a
decorative point of focus—it retains this
role even when the fire is extinguished.
As it is hanging, it also has the benefit of
distributing the heat more evenly and is
more straightforward to install.

A single-loaded corridor was created to act as a buffer between the windows and the bedrooms. Oversized, hinged double-doors open on either side of the living room and invite prevailing winds to flow uninterrupted throughout the interior space.

KAMIQUE

Lee H. Skolnick Architecture + Design Partnership | Anguilla, British West Indies, United Kingdom |
© Thomas Skou, Christian Gomez

The Kamique project is a group of three luxury villas that are linked together in an organic composition along the southern coast of the Caribbean island of Anguilla, in an area known as Little Harbour. The three villas share a panoramic view of the turquoise sea, framed by the spectacular backdrop of the mountains of St. Martin Island in the distance.

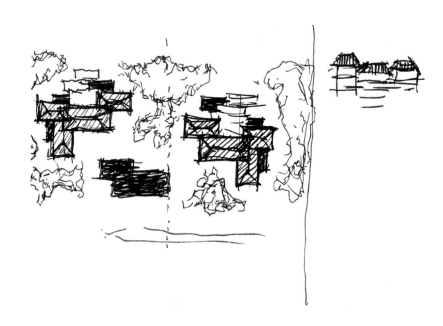

Although the villas vary in size, each one is characterized by three elegant pavilions. The result of this uniformity is a coherent and harmonious style.

122

Each of the villas was individually constructed in order to gain maximum benefit from the ocean views, the natural breeze and the orientation.

123

The dialogue between the interior and the exterior of the villas is reinforced by deep eaves, pergolas and sunshades that create a covered outdoor space.

Floor plan

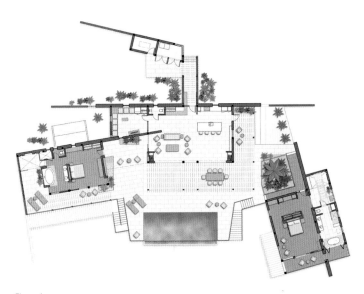

Floor plan

124 Half-height or open-sided walls are useful tools for separating areas without losing either the feeling of space or the light that pours in through the windows that surround the room.

125

The interesting combination of wood, concrete and stone creates a unique architectural mix of modern and traditional.

ANCRAM STUDIO

MOS/Michael Meredith, Hilary Sample | Ancram, New York, United States |
© Michael Vahrenwald

The client for this project wanted a space for both painting and drawing set against an intense landscape of shale cliffs, forest and ponds. The architects sought extreme openness in order to allow the owner to be able to move freely between the mediums of painting and drawing, while at the same time creating space for amenities such as storage, cooking, cleaning and reading. The result is a column-free interior with moment frames on each end, which serve as external porches and viewing spaces between nature and the built environment.

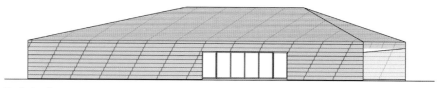

North elevation

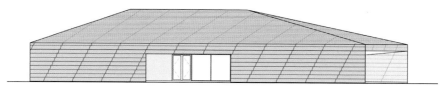

South elevation

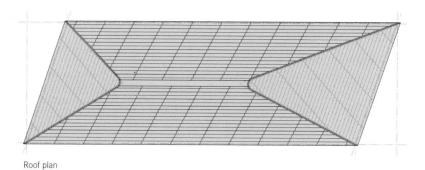

Roof plan

126 A uniform surface of zinc panels clads the facades and roof of the studio. The structural innovation of the building enables the ends to be completely open, full-height glass walls with expansive views toward the landscape.

This project on an isolated site overlooking the hills of Taconic State Park is one of several freestanding structures that make up a compound for an artist and a curator/writer.

127 To create a transition from inside to out and register the transition from the natural surroundings to the interior creative world, the studio is surrounded by a shale perimeter.

Concrete flooring is scored with a geometric pattern that extends the lines from the parallelogram shape of the floor plan.

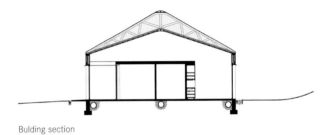

Bulding section

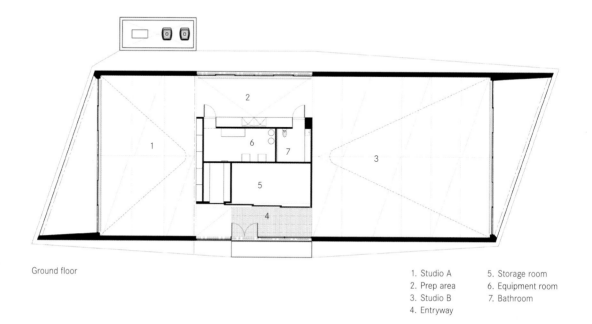

Ground floor

1. Studio A
2. Prep area
3. Studio B
4. Entryway

5. Storage room
6. Equipment room
7. Bathroom

A gray box in the center of the interior contains the kitchen, bathroom and a storage area. Panels that create the walls of the box open and close smoothly by pulling on custom-milled door handles, and reveal archives and a library.

128 Full-height glass walls on either end of the building offer views toward the landscape, while articulated lighting patterns skim over the ceiling to create atmospheric lighting for painting and drawing at night.

HOUSE ON THE CLIFF

Fran Silvestre Arquitectos | Calpe, Spain | © Diego Opazo

Due to the slope of the plot and the desire to contain the home within a single level, the three-dimensional structure of reinforced concrete slabs is adapted to the topography of the chosen site, minimizing movement of the land. The house is on the access level, from which a horizontal platform has been constructed.

129 The cantilevered structure of the building creates the impression that the entire house is a viewing platform onto which the views of the sea are projected. The lighting of the façade emphasizes the architecture and catches the eye from afar.

The concrete structure is insulated from the outside and covered with a flexible soft layer of white lime stucco. The pool is on a lower level, on the flat part of the plot.

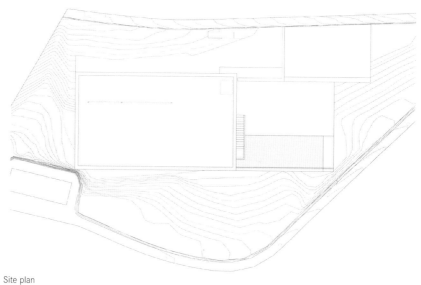

Site plan

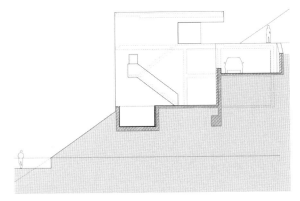

South-west elevation

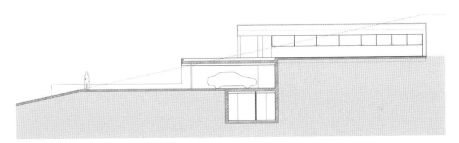

North-west elevation

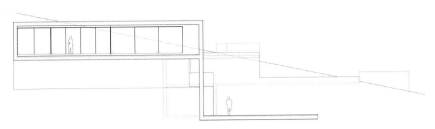

South-east elevation

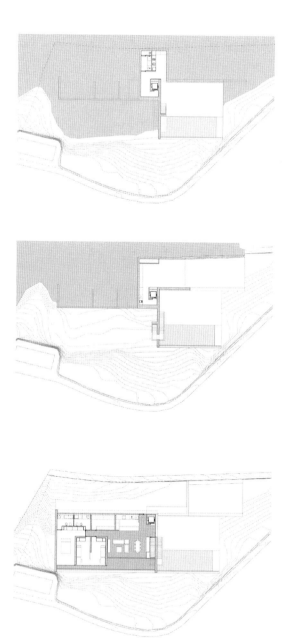

Floor plans

130 An interesting mix of transparencies has been used for the interior of the house. When combined with the uniformity of the white, they provide spectacular light within the space.

131 In keeping with the aesthetics of the rest of the house, a playful mix of white materials has been used for most of the decorative elements. The interior floor is finished in polished marble, the kitchen furniture is finished in white gloss and the worktop is made of Kryon®, an innovative mineral compact whose qualities are perfect for this type of use.

HOUSE COOGEE

JPR Architects | Coogee, Australia | © Brett Boardman

The rustic style of this house has its roots in the Cape Dutch architectural style that is characteristic of the houses in the fishing villages of the west coast of Southern Africa. The design of this house is conceived as a series of bungalows, each with various functions. These are congregated around a courtyard entrance and merge seamlessly with the exterior surroundings.

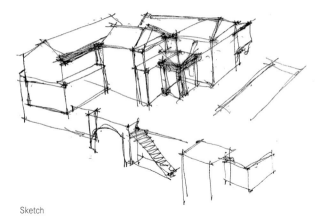

Sketch

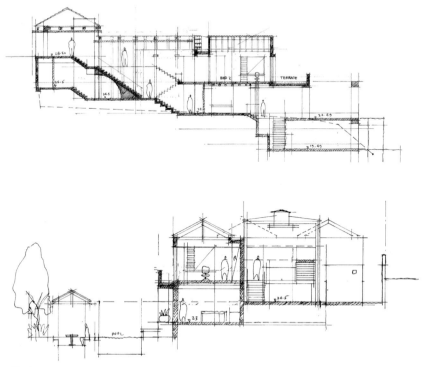

Sections

132 Thanks to the stepped design of the facade, the views can be enjoyed from any of the rooms, all of which are equipped with huge windows and glass doors.

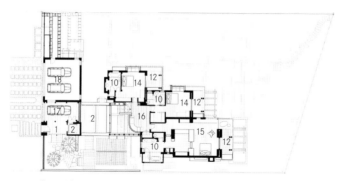

Second floor

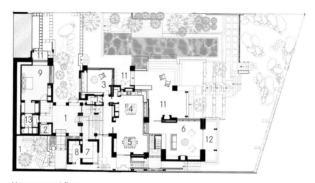

Upper ground floor

Lower ground floor

1. Entrance	11. Deck
2. Lift	12. Balcony
3. Rumpus room	13. Toilet
4. Kitchen	14. Bedroom
5. Dining room	15. Master bedroom
6. Living room	16. Sitting room
7. Office	17. Carport
8. Laundry	18. Garage
9. Guest room	19. Storage room
10. Bathroom	20. Machine room

133 The infinity pool is the centrepiece of this
large terrace, with its waterline that merges
with the horizon and the sea.

134

The lack of artifice, the successful combination of white with the different woods that have been used and the limited color variation create a warm, serene and relaxing space.

A HOUSE IN BRITO

Topos Atelier | Brito, Portugal | © Xavier Antunes

The ruins of an old country home fortuitously placed between a river and a forest of eucalyptus trees were reconstructed and turned into a luxurious modern country home. Though most of the brickwork was demolished for safety reasons, the original stone walls were preserved. The combination of the old rough walls with newer work, including rusted iron panels, creates a surprisingly stunning effect. The surrounding landscape can be enjoyed from around the house thanks to a number of large windows.

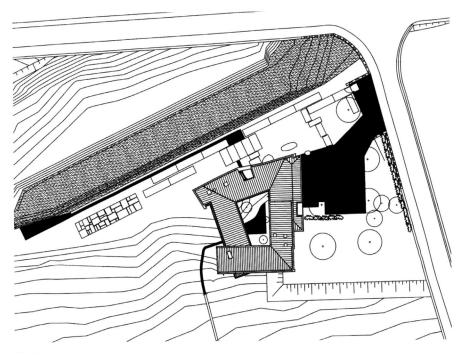

Site plan

laced between a river and a forest of eucalyptus
rees, this country home was restored to its full
lory. The sun reflected on the rusted iron panels
reates a pattern of shades and tones.

135 A number of large windows help cede all attention to the stonework and natural elements surrounding this house in the country.

136 This country house was rebuilt on the natural incline of the terrain. Flights of stairs and staggered slabs of natural granite and concrete help overcome the differences in height.

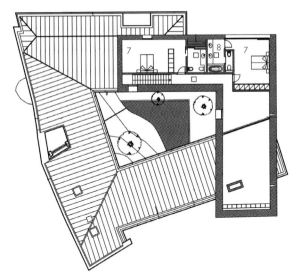

Second floor

Ground floor

1. Entryway
2. Office
3. Kitchen
4. Dining room
5. Lounge
6. Library
7. Bedrooms
8. Bathrooms
9. Utility room
10. Garage
11. Storage
12. Courtyard
13. Garden

137 The living room opens out onto the interior garden on one side and the exterior landscape on the other. The garden is a reflection of the house's surroundings.

FENNEL RESIDENCE

Robert Harvey Oshatz | Portland, Oregon, United States | © Cameron Neilson

This extraordinary floating house artistically captures the curves of the river alongside it. Its architect, Robert Harvey Oshatz, motivated by fluid design, designed a loft-style holiday home. His method involved the creation of a large floating platform manufactured with fir tree trunks to bring stability to the house.

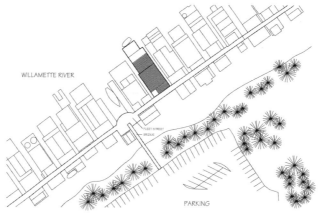

WILLAMETTE RIVER

PARKING

Site plan

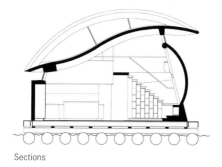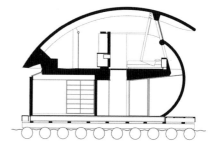

Sections

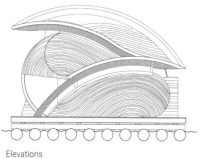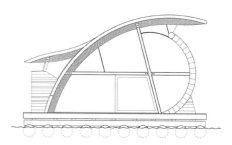

Elevations

138 Different woods were used in the construction and decoration of this house, including Douglas fir Glulam beams to form the gracefully curved ceiling. Every beam has exactly the same radius. The house is topped with copper tiles, a favorite material of the clients who envisioned it weathering with the years and ageing with the house.

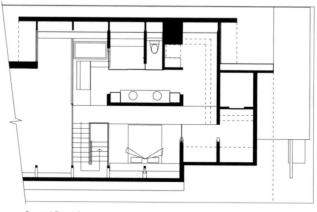

Second floor plan

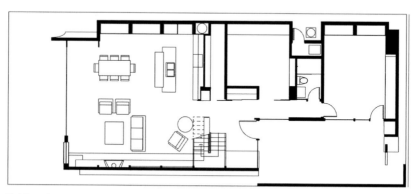

First floor plan

139

The clients wanted a largely open plan interior, requiring no more than a living area, a kitchen, a master suite, a study and a guest bedroom and bathroom. With the floor plan and program established the architect conjured up this inspired design to enclose the space perfectly.

The succession of laminated curves and the beautiful tone of the wood work well with the copper base.

140

The interior is similarly clothed in quality material finishes. Built-in cabinets and storage made of American cherry and Brazilian cherry floors and stairs add a warmth to the house's atmosphere. To complete the look, a floor-to-ceiling glass sliding door opens up onto an uninterrupted vista of the river.

VILLA VRIEZENVEEN

Zecc Architecten | Vriezenveen, The Netherlands | © Cornbread Works

The design of this house, located in the idyllic open and flat Dutch landscape, is inspired by the dark silhouettes of historic farmhouses. This black sculpture is an example of how traditional farmhouses are making way for new artificial or abstract dwellings. Though drastically different on the outside, on the inside this villa follows the linear layout of the traditional farmhouse, with the dining table located in the large living room-cum-kitchen as the center of family life.

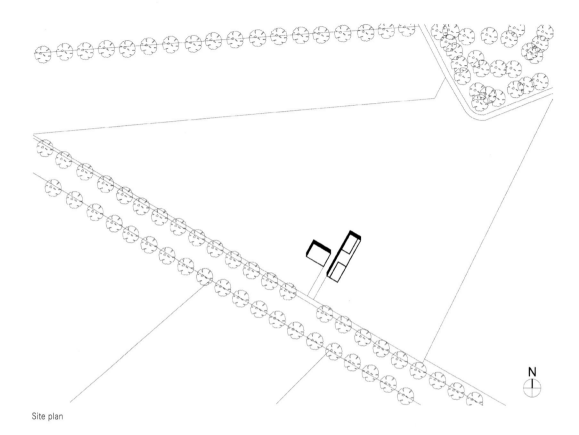

Site plan

141 At first glance it may seem as though this modern villa is out of place in the Dutch countryside, but the black zinc used on the outer walls actually blends in better than the orange rooftops of traditional farmhouses.

Located in the open landscape, which unfolds either side of an ancient country lane, this modern farmhouse follows the linear structure of the Dutch countryside.

142

Three steel portals support two laminate beams, each measuring 3¼ feet high (1 m) and 88½ feet (27 m) long. The walls of the wooden skeleton structure allow overhangs in two directions, creating a carport and covered terrace on either end.

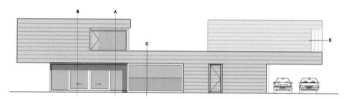

West elevation

North elevation – villa

South elevation – villa

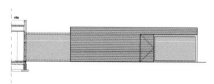

South elevation – extension

North elevation – extension

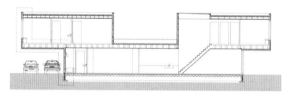

Longitudinal section

The interior of this farmhouse follows the linear
layout of traditional farmhouses. The dining table
in the large living-dining-kitchen is the center of
family life.

143

Traditionally the hub of Dutch houses, the
kitchen in this house is the only room with
multiple orientations and functions. All the
remaining rooms can be accessed from this
central space.

Ground floor

1. Hobby room
2. Storeroom for garden
3. Storeroom for bikes
4. Animals compartment
5. Bedrooms
6. Lounge
7. Storeroom

8. Bathrooms
9. Kitchen
10. Master bedroom
11. Powder room
12. Entryway
13. Carport

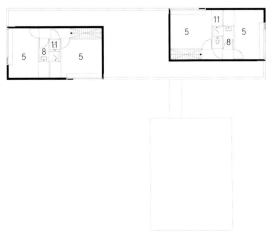

Second floor

All the rooms of this modern Dutch farmhouse have large windows that are oriented towards the surrounding area.

ONE+

add.a.room | The Hague, The Netherlands; Skaane Province, Sweden; and Stockholm, Denmark |
© Add a Room, Matti Marttinen

Just as life itself changes, so too do our housing needs. The concept of a modular house in which
the space can be adapted to what is needed is central to this design of clean and simple lines. The
prefabricated 107-161-215 and 269sq-ft modules (with terrace and pergola) can be joined in a variety
of ways as though it were a game of Lego. The house invites us to play.

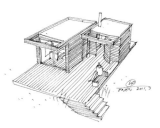

Sauna connected to 161-square-foot
(15 sq m) mini house

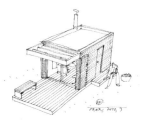

161-square-foot (15 sq m)mini house
with deck and pergola

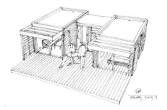

398 square feet (37 sq m). Two modules
connected with linking kitchen or
bathroom module

323-square-foot (30 sq m) mini house
including deck with pergola and outdoor
kitchen module

Two modules 323-square-foot (30 sq m)
mini house in T configuration

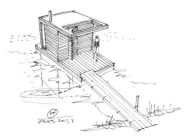

Sauna module

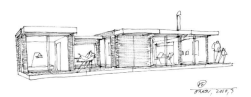

484-square-foot (45 sq m) module assembly
linked to 161-square-foot (15 sq m) module
through deck with pergola

Two 161-square-foot (15 sq m) houses and outdoor
kitchen under pergola

144 By making good use of spacious terraces, you can reduce the need for interior space.

THE AVENEL HOUSE

Paul Morgan Architects | Central Victoria, Australia | © Gollings Photography

The design of this four-bedroom house situated on an extensive terrain in a rural area of Central Victoria—a region known for its intense sun and strong winds—was inspired by the dynamic landscape elements apparent at this exposed countryside setting. The ecological conditions of the site were used to generate formal and spatial qualities in the design. Enormous glass surfaces ensure the landscape can be enjoyed from within while the roof, which seems to wrap itself around the building, protects the interiors from harsh light.

145 The panoramic view over the surrounding
landscape largely determined the design
of this house. A completely transparent
balustrade made of shatterproof glass
borders the terrace.

This home is located in an extensive terrain in a little-inhabited part of the Australian state of Victoria, in a region known for its intense sun and strong winds.

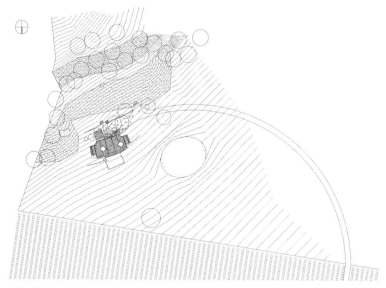

Site plan

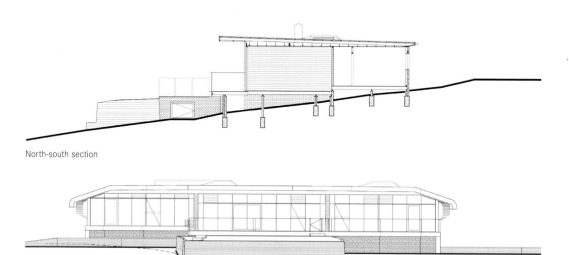

North-south section

Elevation

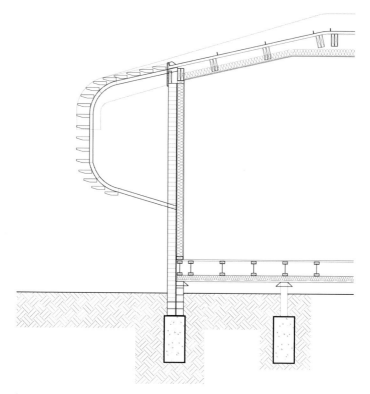

Louver Detail

146 Strathbogie granite was quarried from the site, cut and laid to form a strong relationship between the house and the surrounding landscape.

This house combines a lightweight metal skin with a grounded stone and concrete base. Horizontal wooden slats shade the windows on the narrow side of the house.

147 A protruding roof protects the large floor-to-ceiling windows and interiors from the sun at the hottest time of the day.

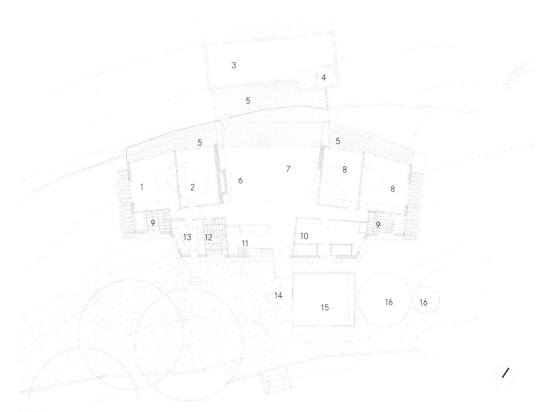

First floor

1. Master bedroom   9. Ensuites
2. Study   10. Play room
3. Pool   11. Kitchen
4. Spa   12. Bathrooms
5. Terrace   13. Laundry room
6. Lounge   14. Courtyard
7. Dining room   15. Shed
8. Bedrooms   16. Water tank

148 Wooden slat windows can control both airflow and the amount of light that enters.

KENSINGTON HOUSE

David Jameson Architect | Kensington, Maryland, United States | © Paul Warchol Photography

The David Jameson Architect studio carried out the renovation of this three-storey house for a young couple. About five miles (eight km) north of Washington, D.C., its modern and minimalist design contrasts with the neighboring post-war era houses.

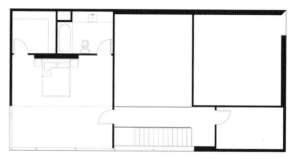

Second floor plan

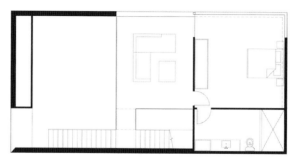

Mezzanine

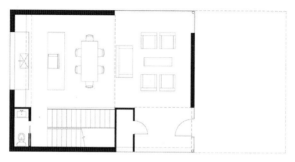

Ground floor plan

149

The functional floorplan reflects the schematic simplicity of the house. The first of the three floors is home to the living room, dining room and kitchen, while the second and third are reserved for the bedrooms.

150 The three levels are connected by a staircase that criss-crosses them in a series of diagonal cuts that slide through the vertical space. White dominates the interior: the walls are white, the ceilings are white and some of the furniture is white. The flooring and the steps of the staircase alone are set off by their rich, dark colour.

The minimalist style of the exterior moves inward, where the various bright rooms develop as a series of interlocking volumes.

TOWNHOUSE

Elding Oscarson | Landskrona, Sweden | © Åke E:son Lindman

Encased in a terrace of period buildings the house, with its smooth, white façade, is an oasis of pure beauty. Although the contrast is strong, the straight lines and simplicity of the white enrich the rhythm of the street. The property is to be used as an art gallery, so the walls are designed not for privacy but for the display of paintings.

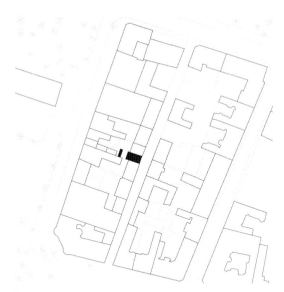

Site plan

Conceptual design

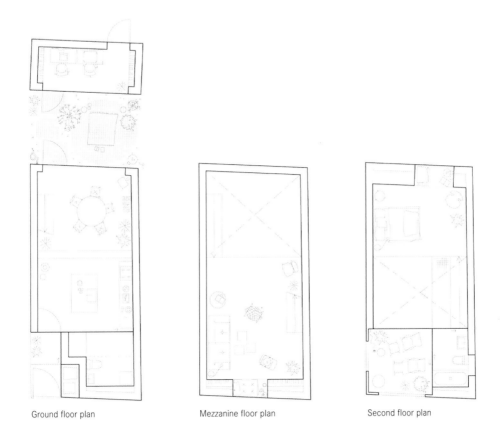

Ground floor plan

Mezzanine floor plan

Second floor plan

151 The use of white, the finish of the floor in joint-free polished concrete and the absence of doors create a feeling of continuity and space within the house.

Open to the skies and the street, the interior is
a juxtaposition of light and welcoming areas; the
layout creates distinct corners here and there for
reading and conversation.

152 The construction of an independent module on the rear terrace to be used as a studio works well. It retains privacy without losing its connection with the rest of the home thanks to the fully glazed wall.

GARCÍA RESIDENCE

Ibarra Rosano Design Architects | Tucson, Arizona, United States | © Bill Timmerman

Situated on a steep north-facing slope in the foothills of the Tucson Mountains, García Residence enjoys commanding views of the surrounding mountains and city lights beyond. After studying the terrain and landscape, the architects discovered the site on which the house was to be constructed is solid rock. The first challenge was to design a structure that seems to rise from the rock without dominating the landscape. The other objective was to create an extraordinary place with ordinary materials.

Situated in one of the world's most dynamic regions, this residence in the foothills of the Tucson Mountains is built on solid rock and the main window is oriented toward the city of Tucson.

153

The axis of the house is set parallel with the site contours, and three narrow bays are created to terrace up the hill, thus keeping excavation and fill to a minimum. The house's three zones—living, circulating and sleeping— are found in the terracing platforms.

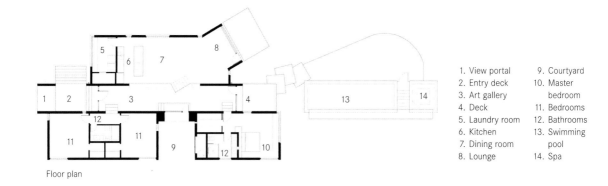

Floor plan

1. View portal
2. Entry deck
3. Art gallery
4. Deck
5. Laundry room
6. Kitchen
7. Dining room
8. Lounge
9. Courtyard
10. Master bedroom
11. Bedrooms
12. Bathrooms
13. Swimming pool
14. Spa

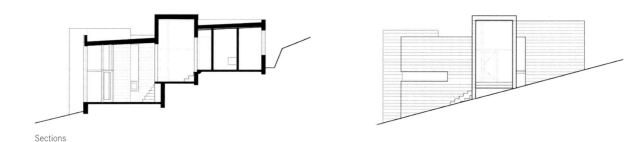

Sections

Situated on a steep, north-facing slope, the architects built three terraces to level out the terrain. Each terrace contains one of the three areas that divide this house: the day area, circulation spaces and a private area.

154

The turning axis of the house allows the inhabitants to enjoy exceptional views from the main window, which is turned toward the city of Tucson. A small interior patio connects the bedrooms and works as an extra room, which provides shade and shelter.

155

A small interior patio connects the bedrooms and functions as an extra room, which provides shade and refuge as well as passive air conditioning for the house in the summer, as the cool air from the mountains passes through the house via the patio.

HOUSE H

Hiroyuki Shinozaki Architects | Chiba, Japan | © Fumihiko Ikemoto

The inward facing Y-shaped wooden beams support the roof and the floorboards of the rooms above. A combination of different materials, such as oak and lime, has been used according to the functionality of the spaces.

156 Framed by a glass wall, the bi-fold glass door also provides light to the whole space, which is free of partitions or walls.

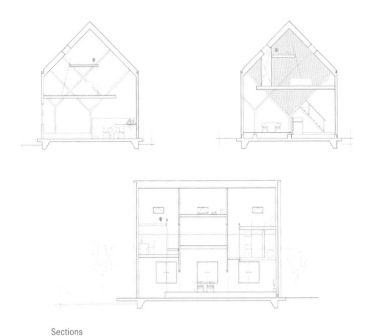

Sections

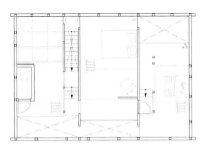

Ground floor plan

Second floor plan

157

The high ceiling is the main protagonist in this house with its classic outer shape. Inside, eight wooden Y-shaped pillars mark the distribution of the space. These pillars come in two distinct forms: with an open top, allowing light to enter whilst still performing a structural function, and with a closed top, creating walls in the upper loft-style level.

158

The original structure is evident in every room of the house, allowing the principally white coloring to combine perfectly with the oak of the columns and beams. Located on the ground floor, the kitchen, dining room and living room are also made of the same material.

159 The wooden staircase with its white sides provides access to the upstairs, separated into islands that define the different bedrooms.

MATAJA RESIDENCE

Belzberg Architects | Malibu, California, United States | © Tim Street-Porter

Situated in an environmentally sensitive area adjacent to a National Park Service area, the site was subject to strict zoning and numerous agency approvals. The rocks on which the house was built greatly influenced the design of the different spaces and the organization of the home; they mark the position of the home and the location of the interior patio, protecting it from the wind and creating some privacy. Some rooms coincide with the rocks, which outline some of the exterior limits.

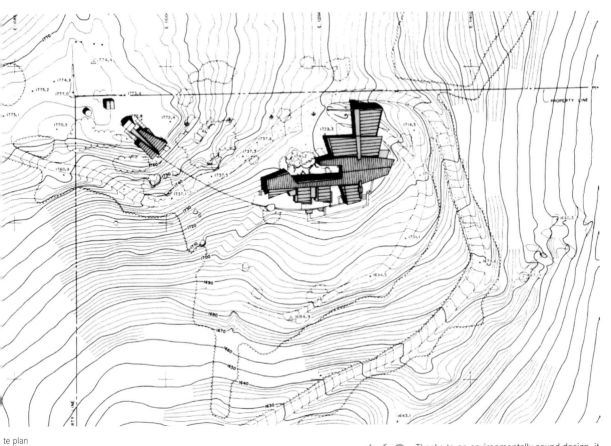

te plan

160 Thanks to an environmentally sound design, it is easy for this construction to be integrated into the landscape. Concrete walls and flooring provide thermal isolation and make it possible for 67 percent of the design to be made of glass.

The metal roof gives the structure a sense of dynamism. The 32-degree inclination serves to catch the sunlight as well as collect rainwater to be used for the irrigation of the lot.

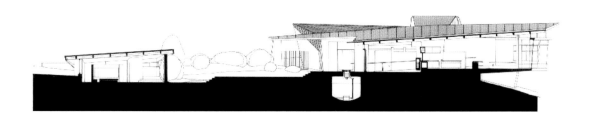

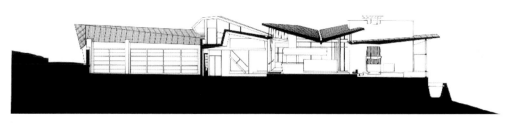

Sections

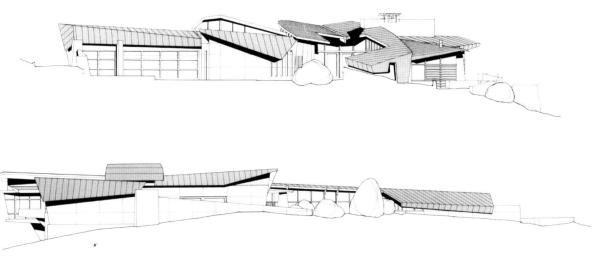

Elevations

161 After carefully considering the plot and the surroundings, the architects created a home with spaces that are situated among the rock formations allowing the whole to blend in naturally with the countryside.

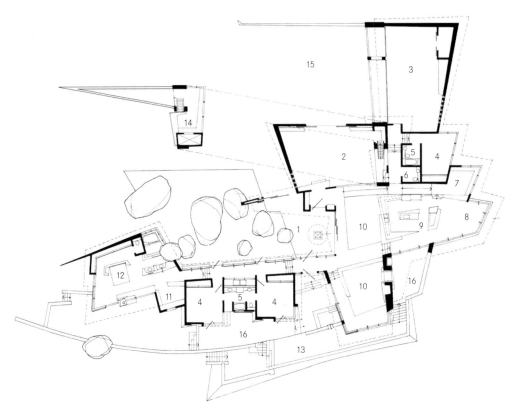

Floor plan

1. Courtyard
2. Automobile gallery
3. Garage
4. Guest room
5. Bathroom
6. Powder room
7. Library
8. Dining room
9. Kitchen
10. Family rooms
11. Offices
12. Master bedroom
13. Pool
14. Carport
15. Decks
16. Balcony

162   The great volume of the rocks combined with the use of large glass panels serve as an exterior limit to some of the house's interior spaces.

The total floor surface of almost 5,000 square feet (465 sq m) houses the main living areas, while an additional 1,000-square-foot (93 sq m) structure contains a garage with three spaces, a guesthouse and a spa and pool, which embody the surroundings.

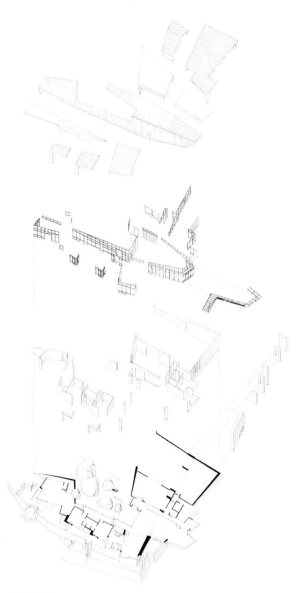

Exploded view

LOW ENERGY BAMBOO HOUSE

Ast 77 | Rotselaar, Belgium | © Jan Liegeois, Marcel Van Coile

The slender stems of organic bamboo that cover the façade produce a visual effect that harmonizes with the nearby trees. The insulation, natural ventilation system and rainwater storage in the basement ensure low energy consumption. The central heating uses a heat pump and underfloor heating.

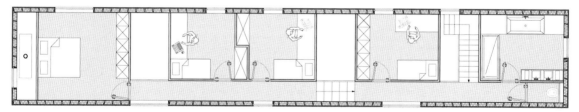

Second floor plan

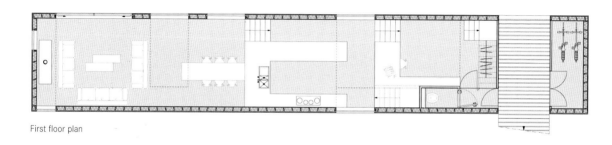

First floor plan

163 The entrance is situated in the underpass, where a balcony offers a view towards the garden and forest. This floor level is an entirely open space. From the entry, one can step down to the kitchen and further descend to the living area and garden level.

164 Strategically placed windows are a source of passive solar heat gain. During the winter period, sunlight is able to heat the interior through the windows after passing through the leafless trees. During the summer, the trees provide a natural sunscreen.

165 Two flights of stairs separate the kitchen and studio from the living room. The same wood has been used for the worktop and the desk in order to give a feeling of continuity to the two spaces.

166 Simple, lightweight, low-rise furniture giving way to large, bare walls has been used to create an airy feeling in the rectangular spaces. Care has also been taken not to clutter the space with too many furnishings.

HILL HOUSE

Johnston Marklee & Associates | Pacific Palisades, California, United States |
© Eric Staudenmaier

This house is the result of the challenge of building a spacious home with views of the Santa Monica Canyon on a small, irregular-shaped lot on an uneven downhill slope. The architects decided to make the base and the upper part of the volume narrower and to enlarge the intermediate level. By doing so, they managed to minimize contact with the natural terrain and to gain square footage thanks to the shape of the concrete, steel and wood structure.

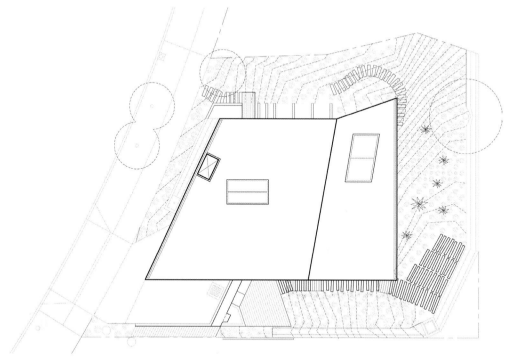

Site plan

The architects faced many challenges in the design of this house: the construction could not exceed 49 feet (15 m), and the surface did not allow for a house of great dimensions.

167 The main facade faces the street and is discreet with few openings. The openings in the facade facing the Canyon maximize views while maintaining privacy. The use of the color white throughout suggests a spatial continuity.

The foundations, built on a base of reinforced concrete pillars, are anchored into the rock and entwined by a network of beams. Inside, the different elements of the domestic program are assembled to blend in with the exterior structure.

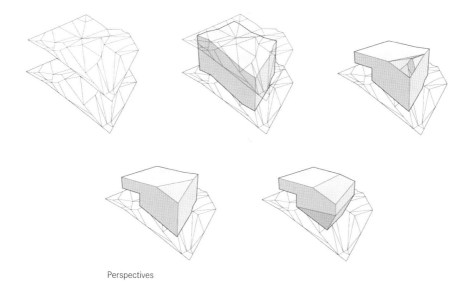

Perspectives

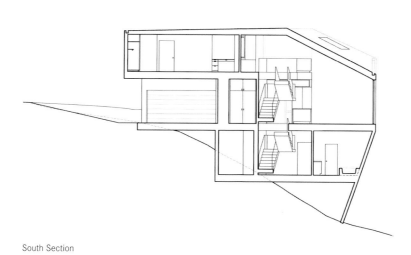

South Section

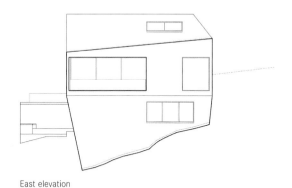

East elevation

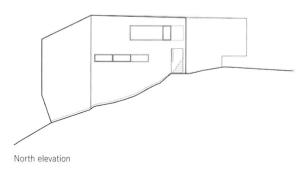

North elevation

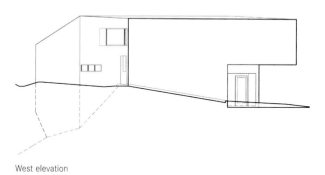

West elevation

South elevation

he day area contains a dining room and kitchen,
semiprivate loft area on the intermediate level
nd an ensuite bedroom on the lower level. A
teel and glass staircase unites these three levels.

Ground floor

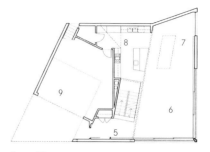

Second floor

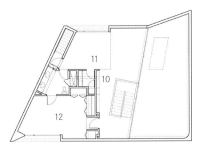

Third floor

1. Sunroom
2. Master bedroom
3. Closet
4. Bathroom
5. Entryway
6. Lounge
7. Dining room
8. Kitchen
9. Garage
10. Library
11. Study
12. Bedroom

White is the main color throughout this house —on the inside and on the outside—and suggests a spatial continuity between the different levels and between the interior and the exterior.

168 To express the continuity of the exterior and blur the difference between the walls and the covering, the architects used a mix of cement and elastomeric material, eliminating the need for a joint sealant.

VILLA RIETEILAND-OOST

Egeon Architecten | Amsterdam, The Netherlands | © Chiel de Nooyer

The geometry of this attractive glass and wooden facade has been planned for practical purposes. The sliding transparent doors on the ground floor are as large as possible in order to maximize the views of the outside and to make access to the garden easy. The second floor windows allow the occupants to choose the degree of seclusion from the exterior. The top floor, fitted out as an office, has panoramic views.

169   If you are lucky enough to have a living room with huge picture windows with views, you need to arrange your furniture so that you can make the most of these views and benefit from the natural light, which is essential for reading and working areas.

170 The choice of wood and warm colours in the decorative details contrasts with the cold gray microcement and creates an atmosphere of warmth.

171

Microcement is a decorative, highly aesthetic and completely waterproof coating. It is a versatile material that provides complete freedom in implementing designs and can be combined easily with other materials. The lack of visible joins lends a sense of continuity to the spaces.

172   A bespoke or plasterboard headboard works well as a decorative element in a bedroom and is very versatile; it can be adapted perfectly to the different spaces. As for the orientation, it should be positioned to one side of the window so that you are not disturbed by the natural light.

173 To make the most of the light without losing privacy, sections of the glass walls in the bathroom have been etched.

DOWNING RESIDENCE

Ibarra Rosano Design Architects | Tucson, Arizona, United States | © Bill Timmerman

Barely discernable from its east-facing mountainside backdrop, the Downing Residence's three split-face block pavilions blend with the surrounding outcroppings, each volume stepping gently within the grove of saguaro that dot the hillside. Each pavilion contains different domestic areas. The kitchen, living and dining rooms are placed beneath a roof that sweeps upward in a butterflylike fashion to maximize the view down to the valley on one side and the towering mountains on the other.

174 The southeast-facing facades have large windows to capture the warm winter sun, while west-facing windows are reduced to the minimum. The house can be opened up to allow the air to circulate and provide a cool and comfortable atmosphere.

Site plan

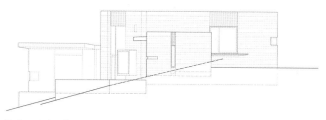

Northeast elevation

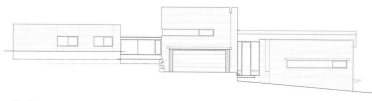

Northwest elevation

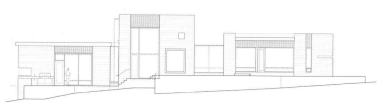

Southeast elevation

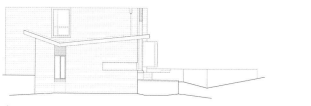

Southwest elevation

The pavilions that make up this structure have
been carefully placed in between the large cacti
and the dense vegetation of the lot.

175 A two-car garage is tucked behind the
pavilion containing the main living space in
order to diminish the impact of garage doors
when approaching the house.

The living room, dining room and kitchen are situated in one of the three volumes that make up this residence, beneath sloping roofs that enhance the views toward the valley on one side and the mountains on the other.

Floor plan

1. Entryway
2. Lounge
3. Dining room
4. Kitchen
5. Pantry
6. Art gallery
7. Powder room
8. Laundry room
9. Workshop
10. Garage
11. Study
12. Master bedroom
13. Pool
14. Library
15. Guest bedroom
16. Weaving studio

176 Rustic materials are chosen to help integrate the building into the landscape. To complement the earthy colors of the house, tinted ashlar, rusted steel, glass, concrete and different types of wood were chosen.

A glass passageway connects the three volumes of this dwelling. The third pavilion contains the master bedroom and a studio. These rooms lead to a large and narrow pool that reflects the landscape.

177 The kitchen is the visual nucleus of the
day area. The materials used are rustic
and natural, and the floor-to-ceiling furniture
incorporates additional storage as well as
heating and cooling systems.

WHITE FALCON

Alberto Rubio Projects | Calvià, Spain | © Oliver Mallah

The design objective of this house was perhaps an unusual one. The aim was to create a home in the shape of a bird with outstretched wings, giving the impression that it was about to take off in flight. The building is located on a sandstone cliff and it was this natural setting that ultimately defined the form of the "bird house."

178 The distribution of space is determined by
the topography. The gardens are on the
right at the front while the pool, a symbol of
vacations, is positioned in the central area,
adding colour, freshness and sound. In winter
it is a magnificent source of light, with the
pool becoming a lamp in an inverted sky,
where the bird is reflected.

The distribution of the different rooms is defined
to a great extent by the topography of this plot of
land that is located so close to the cliff top.

SORRENTO HOUSE

Archiblox | Sorrento, Victoria, Australia | © Tom Ross, Brilliant Creek

This was the project of a couple with grown-up children who needed an extra house to accommodate family and guests. They hired a firm of architects for the job, who designed, manufactured and installed this modular house in just 15 weeks. Bathed in natural light, this house is characterized by being completely open to the outside. But only when the mosquito screen is not needed!

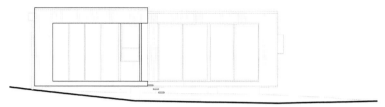

North elevation

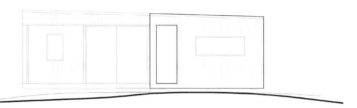

West elevation

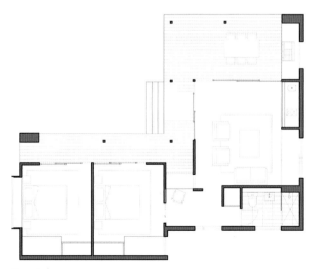

Floor plan

The house is notable for its great insulation thanks to its locks and double-glazed windows. It also incorporates a gray-water treatment system.

179 Sliding doors with mosquito nets are a good way of providing protection from insects in the summer while enjoying the breeze outside.

180

It is a good idea to use the same type of materials in small houses in order to maximize the feeling of continuity and harmony within the space. Use pieces of furniture or decorative elements as a point of contrast to break up the uniformity of the colors and materials.

CLIFF HOUSE

Khosla Associates | Chowara, India | © Bharath Ramamrutham

Located on the coast of the Arabian Sea, this house is perched on the edge of a cliff top in the wide, green strip of a coconut plantation. The property's most prominent feature is undoubtedly its large, sloping, asymmetric roof. This triangular roof structure is supported by a 147-foot (45 m) long oblique wall, which creates a projection of light over the extensive views.

Thanks to its position and elongated shape, the large infinity pool compensates for the fact that the house lacks direct access to the beach.

Long section

181   Wide beams were built into the main roof especially to provide protection from the intense sun and monsoon rains.

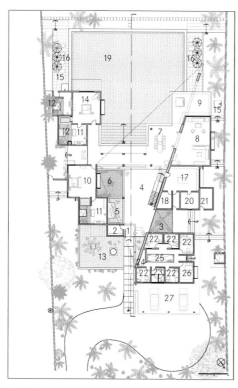

Ground floor

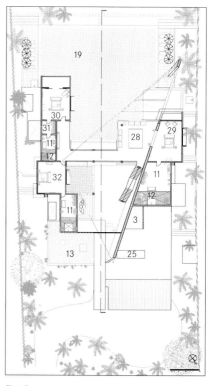

First floor

1. Entrance	12. Shower	23. Staff bathroom
2. Cloak room	13. Pond	24. Machine room
3. Garden	14. Bedroom	25. Patio
4. Hall	15. Shower	26. Staff kitchen
5. Pond	16. Deck	27. Garage
6. Garden	17. Kitchen	28. Meditation deck
7. Dining room / Deck	18. Cellar	29. Master bedroom
8. Living room	19. Pool	30. Bedroom
9. Deck	20. Laundry	31. Dressing room
10. Bedroom	21. Pool room	32. Bedroom
11. Bathroom	22. Staff room	

182

In order to keep the views and create a comfortable environment in the tropical Kerala heat, it was essential that all the spaces had plenty of openings in order to facilitate the movement of the seasonal winds.

183 Using large expanses of glass to seal the gaps would trap the heat in this environment, so a system of sliding and folding wooden shutters was designed for the doors and windows. These venetian blinds can be adjusted to allow the breeze to flow through freely.

184

The external and internal finishes are polished cement, concrete and rough slate juxtaposed against warm slatted timber and natural local kota stone. Furniture and accessories are kept to a minimum, so as not to distract from the beauty of the natural surroundings.

PREFAB HOUSE IN DENMARK

ONV Arkitekter | Gilleleje, Denmark | © Per Johansen, Station 1

The aim of this project was to build an architectural, quality house at an affordable price. The standard prefabricated house has a minimalist design. The facade of this house is clad in Siberian larch and glass, while the interior walls are covered in drywall. The residence is available in six basic configurations, which can be adapted to the customer's specific needs and expanded with additional prefabricated segments. Moreover, louvers can be installed on the facade to either block the sun in the dining area or shelter the terrace and create a room for outdoor living.

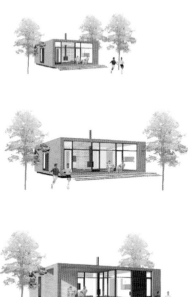

Rendered perspective

185 This minimalist residence is available in six configurations, which can be adapted to meet the individual's needs for space and function by combining the built modules in different ways and adding modules to expand the whole.

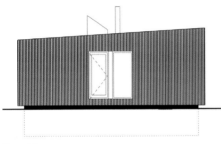

Ground floor

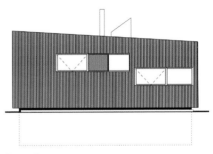

Ground floor

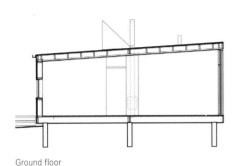

Ground floor

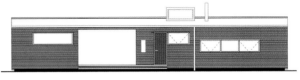

Ground floor

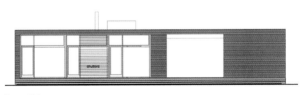

Ground Floor

The wood-stud facade is clad with Siberian larch.
Each floor plan is centered around a large space that
accommodates the living and dining areas and an
open kitchen that can be adjoined to the verandah.

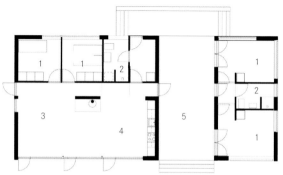

Ground floor

1. Bedrooms
2. Bathrooms
3. Lounge
4. Kitchen/dining room
5. Porch

186 The interior of this minimalist residence is dominated by open rooms. The kitchen, dining room and living room have been combined into a spacious living area that invites plenty of light and air.

BLAIRGOWRIE HOUSE

Archiblox | Blairgowrie, Victoria, Australia | © Tom Ross, Brilliant Creek

The owners of this property wanted to create a carefree vacation home close to the beach. The aim was to build a single-floor house with large common areas that was open to the outside. Three modules were used to create an asymmetric H form, maximizing on the northern orientation of this Australian house to draw plenty of light inside, even in the winter.

East elevation

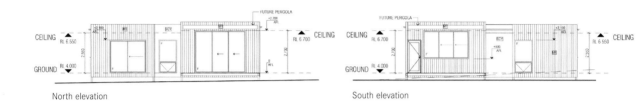

North elevation

South elevation

West elevation

Floor plan

Inside, the floor-to-ceiling walls are clad in wood. The large north-and south-facing windows provide plenty of cross ventilation.

187 The design of this house can be defined as sustainable as it has adopted various energy-saving principles such as positioning the living areas on the north side, cross ventilation, high levels of insulation, double glazing, effective seals and protection from the sun.

188 The kitchen island fulfils three functions: it acts as a work area, a breakfast bar and a room divider.

189 Black and dark gray have been used predominantly on the furnishings and decorative details to provide a contrast with the wooden cladding that is used throughout the house, providing a link with the colour of the exterior façade.

190 Depending on the level of privacy you want to achieve, you can shun the traditional approach of closing the shower area and gain a lot of space in the process. Do take care, however, with the positioning of the showerhead and drain to avoid flooding or making your bathroom fittings or accessories wet.

HOUSE #19

Korteknie Stuhlmacher Architecten, Bik Van der Pol (Artists) | Utrecht, The Netherlands |
© Mechthild Stuhlmacher, Rien Korteknie, Christian Kahl

In 2004, within the framework of the art organization Beyond, the municipality of Utrecht invited several international artists to live and work for a limited period of time in a newly built city extension, the Leidsche Rijn, to observe and react to the growing and rapidly changing place from various perspectives. Part of the municipal program, House #19 is a mobile studio, that will change location several times during the course of the planned activities. The house consists of one long space, which can be divided into interior and exterior spaces.

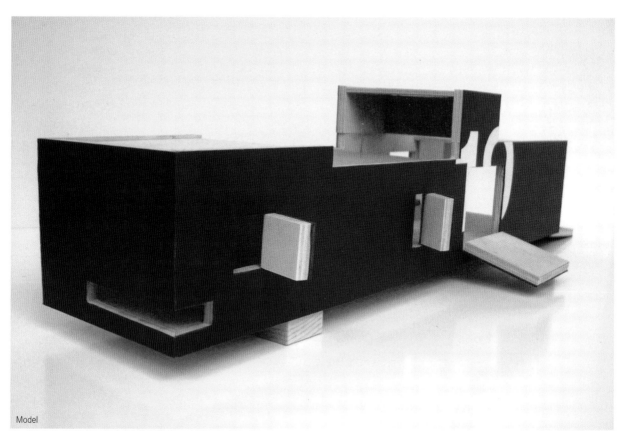

Model

191 Consisting of one long space, this house adapts to the inhabitants' needs. It can be a hotel, exhibition space, studio or hospitable dwelling with a large table, plenty of daylight and all the privacy required.

Despite its mobility, this construction is large,
robust and durable. The construction is simple:
the walls, floor and roof are entirely made of
wooden panels fixed with steel joints. The whole
is strong enough to be transported in one piece.

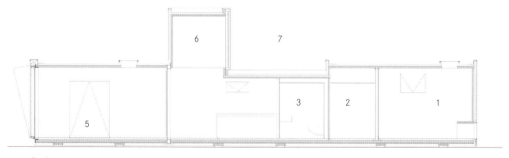

Section

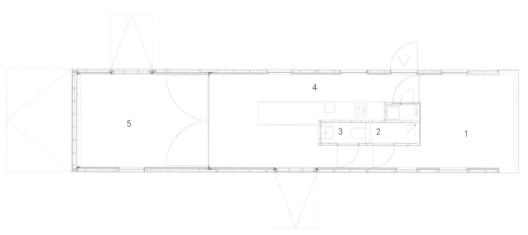

Ground floor

1. Bedroom   5. Powder room
2. Storage   6. Lounge
3. Kitchen   7. Roof terrace
4. Shower room

The rectangular floor plan contains a bedroom, shower, powder room, kitchen, living room, studio and roof terrace and can be adapted to the individual needs of each inhabitant.

192 The walls, floor and roof of this simple construction are made of solid laminated sheets of European softwood and are stabilized by two steel frames. The object is sturdy, heavy and environmentally sound.

193 The wooden interior blends in with the surroundings when the shutters are folded out, and the house has a completely different character, as these turn into terraces, ramps or platforms.

TREEHOUSE RIGA

Appleton e Domingos Arquitectos | Anywhere | © Fernando Guerra, FG+SG

Building a simple and restrained modular home does not need to compromise the beauty of its lines, as this example highlights. Composed of two 237-square-foot (22 sq m) modules, this home takes up very little space yet it boasts a living area with kitchen, two bedrooms, a bathroom and two outdoor patios. With time, finish and price on their side, modular homes offer all we need.

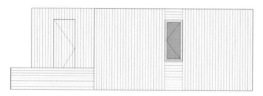

Side elevation

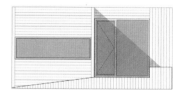

Front elevation

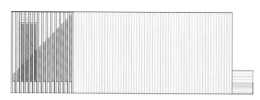

Side elevation

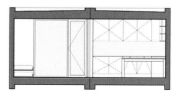

Back elevation

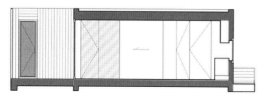

Section A

Section B

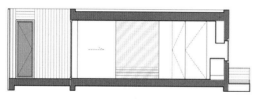

Section A'

194 Two modules of some 215 square feet (20 sq m), each containing a living room with kitchenette and two small bedrooms—one double and one for children or guests—and sharing a bathroom. A birch-wood wall / sliding door provides the versatility to create two completely different homes, one for the day and one for the night, according to need.

195 One of the patios is open while the other is closed. They also have different orientations in order to make the most of the outside space at any given time.

196 The house's small size leads its architects to define it with large glazed closures so as to provide magnificent views of the surrounding landscape and create a greater feeling of space in the building.

197

The cheery and cozy atmosphere of a
Mediterranean house was the inspiration
for the architect when he planned his
design. Although it contrasts with the Nordic
environment that is usually associated with
a traditional tree house, the Mediterranean
environment is also connected with the
concept of the house.

The Thermowood patio floors provide continuity
with the Riga wood of the interior floors,
while drawing the house visually closer to its
surrounding environment.

WATERSHED

Float Architectural Research and Design | Willamette Valley, Oregon, United States |
© J. Gary Tarleton

The first request of the client of this small writing studio (just 100 square feet/9.3 sq m) was to have a roof that would let her hear the rain falling. The writing studio she calls her Watershed sits on a small piece of land along the Marys River, just uphill from riparian wetlands, and is designed to reveal the ecological complexity of the site to visitors. Thus, rare reptiles and amphibians can be observed through a floor-level window, while the roof diaphragm amplifies rain sounds and a water collection basin not only measures past rainfall but doubles as a step and attracts birds and deer.

198 This small writing studio in the Willamette Valley, Oregon, was constructed without road access, without electricity on site and without major excavation. Moreover, the building is 100 percent removable and recyclable.

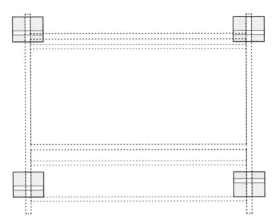

Foundation plan

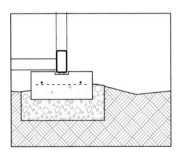

Foundation at corner

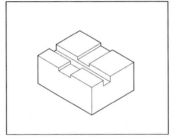

Footer

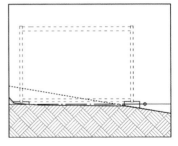

Site elevation

199 The first stage of construction was the site-poured foundation piers that are cast to spread the weight of the building on the ground and to drain water away from the steel frame, which was shop fabricated and dropped in a single piece onto the piers by a track-drive front loader.

There are no irreversible connections in the construction of this shed. The wood enclosure can be updated or recycled as necessary and the steel frame can be removed and reused or recycled.

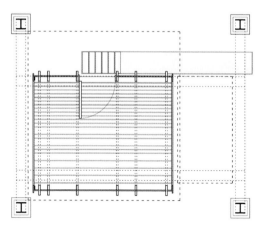

Site plan

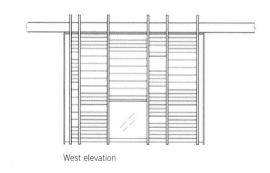

West elevation

East elevation

Stainless steel bolts connect dado-grooved cedar two-by-sixes to a steel frame. The final tongue-in-groove cedar-and-glass enclosure layer floats in the grooves and on rubber engine seats.

200

The construction of this studio, which is completely removable and recyclable, was possible despite lack of road access and on site electricity and was completed without major excavation.

HOUSE K

Stephan Maria Lang | Seeshaupt, Germany | © Hans Kreye, Viewtopia

The owners of this property had dreamt for a long time of possessing their very own lakeside home, which was in total harmony with its natural environment. This dream was achieved by recreating a coastal landscape with careful architectural interventions. The construction itself conjures up the image of a boathouse or even perhaps a Scandinavian church.

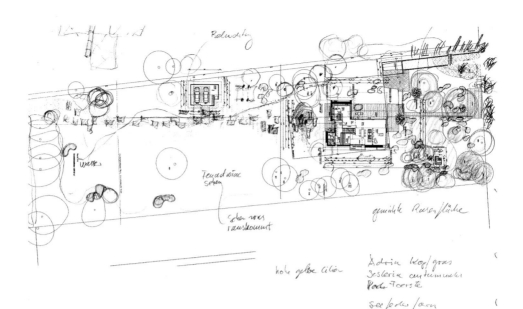

Site plan sketch

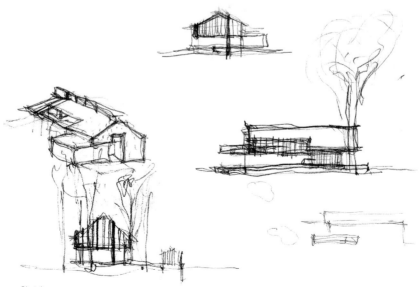

Sketch

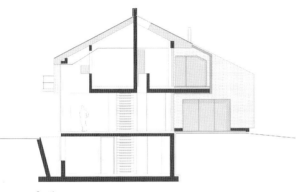

Section

201 The building appears to be composed of two shells, pierced by a shaft of light. This line begins in the driveway, continues through the building and ends in the lake.

202 In a minimalist space, with straight-lined furniture and an absolute predominance of white, a central fireplace adds warmth as well as an interesting colour contrast.

1. Living room
2. Dining room
3. Office
4. Kitchen
5. Pantry
6. Entrance
7. Toilet
8. Storage room
9. Terrace

Ground floor

1. Bedroom
2. Bathroom
3. Dressing room
4. Light well
5. Office
6. Guest room
7. Bathroom
8. Hallway
9. Porch
10. Balcony

First floor

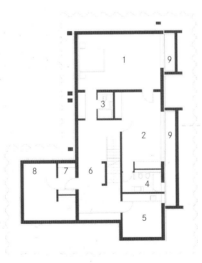

1. Guest room
2. Guest room
3. Bathroom
4. Bathroom
5. Laundry
6. Hallway
7. Cellar
8. Machine room
9. Light well

Basement floor